GRANDPARENTING IN DIVORCED FAMILIES

Neil Ferguson

with Gillian Douglas, Nigel Lowe, Mervyn Murch
and Margaret Robinson

First published in Great Britain in January 2004 by

The Policy Press
University of Bristol
Fourth Floor
Beacon House
Queen's Road
Bristol BS8 1QU
UK

Tel +44 (0)117 331 4054
Fax +44 (0)117 331 4093
e-mail tpp-info@bristol.ac.uk
www.policypress.org.uk

British Library Cataloguing in Publication Data
A catalogue record for this book is available from the British Library

Library of Congress Cataloging-in-Publication Data
A catalog record for this book has been requested

ISBN 1 86134 498 8 paperback

A hardcover version of this book is also available

Neil Ferguson is a Research Associate in the Cardiff Family Studies Research Centre, Cardiff Law School, Cardiff University, UK.

Cover design by Qube Design Associates, Bristol.
Front cover: photograph supplied by kind permission of Taxi.
Printed and bound in Great Britain by Hobbs the Printers Ltd, Southampton.

Contents

Acknowledgements

We would like to express our thanks to the many people who made this research possible. We are grateful to the grandparents, parents and children who gave their time to be interviewed and who provided a great deal of information about family relationships. The names of family members have been changed to ensure that individuals cannot be identified.

We are also grateful to the Lord Chancellor's Department which supported our research and provided us with access to divorce files in the courts. Thanks must also go to the managers in the courts in Bristol, Cardiff, Newport and Swansea who allowed the research team to study court files and who contacted parents by post on the project's behalf.

The authors are indebted to Kay Bader (a former member of the research team) who conducted some of the interviews and typed some of the interview transcripts, and to Zafar Khan who provided IT support for the project. We are also grateful to Lynn Chesterman, the Director of the Grandparents' Association, for her interest in this book. The project's Advisory Committee (Professor Douglas Hooper, Sharon Witherspoon, Professor Hilary Land, Professor Geoff Dench, Dr Christine Piper, Frances Hunt, and representatives from the Home Office and the Lord Chancellor's Department) are thanked for their support and advice.

Finally, we are most grateful to the Nuffield Foundation – the sponsors of our research – for its support. Without the Nuffield Foundation's funding, the research on which this book is based could not have been undertaken.

Neil Ferguson, Gillian Douglas, Nigel Lowe,
Mervyn Murch and Margaret Robinson
(The research team)

ONE

Introduction

This is a book about grandparents whose sons or daughters have divorced. It discusses the findings of a two-year interdisciplinary research study at Cardiff University. The project was supported by a grant from the Nuffield Foundation and the research was completed in May 2001. The project set out to explore family members' perceptions of the impact of divorce on grandparenting. The study was designed to provide a tri-generational perspective and information was gathered from interviews with parents, children and maternal and paternal grandparents. In this chapter we aim to provide a description of the research and explain why we believe it is important to discover more about grandparents' roles in divorced families.

Introduction

The breakdown of a marriage usually involves major readjustments for parents and children and a realignment of the network of contacts with friends and family. Mothers may need to make changes to the once familiar pattern of daily life and this often involves recruiting grandparents to provide support. Researchers have commented on the establishment of 'matrilineal' families, or what Aldous (1995, p 108) describes as "the female tilt in the kinship structure". This refers to the marked tendency of mothers, children and maternal grandparents to form close alliances. Following a divorce, the mother normally becomes the resident parent (the parent responsible for the day-to-day care of the children), and the paternal grandparent connection is likely to break should fathers fail to maintain contact and keep the connection alive. Maternal grandparents who may have seen themselves as a latent resource during the marriage (see Riley and Riley, 1993) find themselves called into service when their daughter and son-in-law decide that they no longer want to live together. Bengtson (2001, p 5) concluded that "For many Americans, multigenerational bonds are becoming more important than nuclear family ties for well-being and support over the course of their lives". The process of negotiating post-divorce parenthood is rarely easy because most parents are ill prepared for the changes (Smart and Neale, 1999). When help is needed, parents often turn to their own parents. Our project investigated the role that grandparents play in families and the effect of parental divorce on their relationships with grandchildren.

Why did we choose to study grandparents?

Grandparenthood can be an important part of the lifecycle, and the increased longevity and health of the older generation in the UK has meant that school-aged children are likely to have grandparents. Oeppen and Vaupel (2002) have studied life expectancy in the UK (currently 75.0 years for men and 79.9 years for women) and have noted that it has increased every year since 1840. These authors concluded that there is no natural limit and we should assume that life expectancy will continue to rise for the foreseeable future.

In the US, Uhlenberg and Kirby (1998, p 25, table 2.1) have noted that around three quarters of the population of 30-year-olds have at least one grandparent. Almost 10% of 20-year-olds still have all of their grandparents compared with only 3% in 1960. One reason why intergenerational relationships currently generate greater interest from researchers is that there are more grandparents in the population.

There is also a widely held view that grandparents often have an important influence on their grandchildren's upbringing and may remain significant people in their adult grandchildren's lives (Mills et al, 2001). The intergenerational transmission of knowledge and values (Kennedy, 1992), a sense of family heritage and stability (Kornhaber, 1996) and guidance on childcare practices (Szinovacz, 1998) are among the benefits that have been attributed in the research literature to grandparenting. In Chapter Two, we review research into the characteristics of grandparents and the part that grandparents play within the wider family. It is sufficient, at this point, to note that one important reason for studying grandparents is the belief that they can have an important influence on family values, traditions and childcare practices.

Just over a decade ago, it was considered likely that one marriage in three was likely to end in divorce and that one in five children was likely to experience the divorce of their parents. This prospect has now become a reality and there is an expectation of further increases in the proportion of marriages that will ultimately fail. The Family Policy Studies Centre (2000) provided an account of the rate of family change in the UK in the 21st century. It predicted that, in the near future, just over two in every five marriages will ultimately end in divorce and that more than a quarter of the child population will have to cope with the divorce of their parents before they reach their 16th birthday. An increase in the incidence of family break-up, whether the result of divorce or the separation of married or unmarried parents, means that grandparents are more likely to be called upon to provide support for parents and grandchildren in the aftermath of parental separation. This study's emphasis on *divorced families* makes a contribution to an aspect of grandparenting that has been under-researched in the UK.

One of the objectives of our study was to consider whether grandparents are important to their grandchildren. A view of the importance of grandparenting, its diversity and its functions can be helpful in coming to conclusions about grandparents' rights to legal recognition. Does the testimony of grandparents, of grandparents, parents and grandchildren lead us to believe that grandparents deserve a special position in family life that ought to be recognised in law? Should we support the view of the Grandparents' Association and other pressure groups that campaign for grandparents' rights? Should grandparents be given special consideration when a court is deciding how children should be looked after when their parents have died or are unable or unwilling to provide adequate care?

Grandparents and public policy

Current government policy is to encourage women with dependent children to go out to work in order to shift them from dependency upon means-tested welfare benefits to at least partial financial independence (topped up with tax credits and child support from the fathers of their children) (Douglas, 2000; Mumford, 2001). Many women in this target group have young children who require childcare and those who are separated and divorced are likely to need financial support. In its consultation paper, *Supporting families* (Home Office, 1998), the government recognised grandparents' potential role as childcarers. The Department for Work and Pensions has also been reported to be considering paying grandparents to provide childcare for single parents so that they would be able to return to work (Arthur et al, 2002). There have been suggestions about training grandparents (Strom and Strom, 1991), and providing them with advice services to enable them to fulfil their roles more effectively (Home Office, 1998; Richards, 2001, p 105). However, the choices that grandparents make about the future path of their own lives do not always sit comfortably with policies aimed at mobilising them nationally as supporters of the wider family. *Supporting families* assumes that grandparents want to provide help for their adult children and grandchildren. The paper argues that they play a significant role in supporting their families and it is one that the government wishes to promote (see Chapter Seven of this book). The Home Office appears to be suggesting that, when circumstances allow, grandparents can and perhaps should provide the childcare that will allow some parents to achieve the shift from dependence on benefits to full or part-time employment. But, this is part of a wider aim to persuade 'older people' (see p 15) to assume an enhanced role in supporting children. The consultation document suggests, for example, that health visitors should encourage the involvement of the wider family and it asks for advice (see p 15) about "the best way to involve grandparents in children's education and how best to involve older volunteers in schools".

However, some contemporary grandparents may believe that they have fulfilled their obligations to their families and to society when they have completed the upbringing of their own children. It is, in their view, the next generation's turn to assume the family responsibilities with which most grandparents are only too familiar. It might be concluded that family life, in intact as well as divorced families, is becoming increasingly fragmented. It is a view that has attracted the attention of sociologists (see Giddens, 1992) who argue that social transformations, including processes of individualisation, have made inroads into more traditional values that emphasised the needs of the family group. Beck and Beck-Gernsheim (2002) argue that men and women no longer place the same emphasis on merging their interests, submerging their aspirations or seeing the need to compromise for the sake of their relationship. The pursuit of individual goals has meant that children do not have as much power to constrain their parents' life choices (Jensen, 2003), and increased freedom for adults may often be bought at the expense of a lack of security for children. We may now live in a world characterised by "long term family transformations, where adults are in charge of agency and where children's symbolic power is lost" (Jensen, 2003, p 146). Have there been similar changes in grandparents' relationships with parents and grandchildren? Is it fair for the government to expect more of grandparents or encourage parents and others to believe that grandparents should improve the effectiveness of their family support role? Our study of grandparenting in divorced families was intended to shed light on the answers to these questions.

Introduction to the study

Our study aimed to contribute more generally to knowledge of the roles and functions of grandparenting and to investigate the support that grandparents provide for parents and grandchildren. Its objectives were:

1. to explore the nature of the grandchild–grandparent relationship and the effects on that relationship of parental divorce;
2. to examine the nature of the support that parents and grandchildren receive from maternal and paternal grandparents after the breakdown of marriage;
3. to explore the differences (if any) between the grandparenting of grandmothers and grandfathers and the nature of maternal and paternal grandparents' relationships with their grandchildren;
4. to explore the effects of grandchild and grandparent age on the grandparent–grandchild relationship;
5. to describe grandparents' reactions to their adult child's divorce, their 'partisan' behaviour and its effects on the divorced family;
6. to discuss the legal position of grandparents after parental divorce;
7. to investigate grandchildren's contact with grandparents before and after divorce;
8. to describe how communications between the two sides of divorced families are managed across the generations;
9. to discuss, in the light of the evidence, whether grandchildren think that their relationships with their grandparents are important.

Table 1: The family members who were interviewed

	Mothers	Fathers	Children	Maternal grand-parent	Paternal grand-parent	Total
Divorced in 1997	22	9	20	11	8	70
Divorced in 2000	11	7	10	10	7	45
Total	33	16	30	21	15	115

The evidence was gathered from a study of the interview transcripts of 115 family members in 44 families who were drawn at random from the court files of couples who had been granted decree nisi in the first half of 1997 and 2000. Table 1 contains information about the numbers of parents, grandparents and grandchildren who took part in the study.

Qualitative data analysis

Two members of the research team (one male and one female) interviewed family members. All interviews were transcribed in full and each transcription was analysed using the computer programme ATLAS.ti (see the Appendix). Our analysis aimed to determine whether specific predictions generated *within* the data held up when they were tested across a larger number of cases. The process also supported the development of 'Grounded Theory' (see Glaser and Strauss, 1968) in the sense that issues were generated from the text rather than imposed as the result of some external body of theory.

The analysis aimed to identify recurring themes and issues that emerged from the interview data. For example, when only a handful of interviews had been analysed, some families were identified in which the maternal grandparents had become heavily involved with childcare duties, and it was observed that these committed grandparents often expressed reservations about the extent of their involvement. As a result, the interview questions about childcare aimed to discover whether parents were aware of grandparents' reservations and whether grandparents had discussed their concerns with parents. This is just one example of a theme that was 'grounded in the utterances of the informants' and identified as a result of qualitative data analysis.

The interviews began by asking: 'What is your family situation at the moment?'. This was effective in encouraging family members to talk about family life in conversations that were not entirely predictable. Respondents did not always comment on the same topics but rather talked about the issues that they felt were important. Interview guides (see Appendix, Table A3) ensured that each of the interviewers who completed the fieldwork covered the same ground. Although the transcripts have been searched on occasions to count the numbers of family members who expressed a particular point of view, this was not intended to be a statistical study. It was exploratory research that applied qualitative research methods to analyse the interview transcripts (see

Miles and Huberman, 1994). The methodology and the approach are described in the Appendix that we have included in this book.

Strengths and limitations of the study

It was particularly important to talk to grandchildren, as many of the assumptions about the value and importance of grandparents to their grandchildren in previous studies have come from grandparents or parents or from the recollections of adult grandchildren (Mills et al, 2001; Roberto et al, 2001). It was also important to generate data that was authentic and rich in detail, and this study succeeded in gathering accounts of the stories that family members had to tell about their experiences of grandparenting and divorce. Large-scale surveys, as we observe in Chapter Two, cannot always provide this perspective.

Qualitative research, however, raises concerns about a lack of objectivity in interpreting respondents' statements, and the reliability of the findings. This study did not set out to be all-embracing. It did not collect material that would allow us to comment on trends in grandparenting or the effects of the passage of time on the changing perceptions of the families that took part in the study. No Asian or African Caribbean parents accepted our invitation to take part in the research and the sample is small and not representative of the general population. Only one grandchild (aged 8-16) in each family was interviewed. We also discovered the task of tracing a highly mobile group of divorced parents and persuading them to take part in the research to be particularly challenging.

About one in six of the parents whose names were obtained from court files (see Appendix) agreed to be interviewed and, in most cases, one parent in each divorced couple gave consent. Many did not want to talk to a researcher about their divorce and its effect on their own and their children's relationships with the wider family and most did not reply to the letter of invitation. Considerable efforts were made to follow up parents who did not respond, but these were often unsuccessful. Some of those who were telephoned said that they were "just not interested". Others now had new partners and spouses and felt that the time had come "to move on" and "put this behind me". Some were concerned about upsetting their children and others did not welcome the fact that both sides of the divorced family might be interviewed. Some parents said that they were afraid of upsetting their ex-spouses who might be angry when they learned that their marriage and divorce had been discussed with a researcher. It seemed to be difficult to talk to representatives of both sides of the divided family, particularly when there was evidence of continuing acrimony after a divorce. It was recognised from the outset that the research was sensitive and intrusive, likely to include families in which there was continuing acrimony and that a high number of refusals was probable. Other researchers in the field (Arthur et al, 2002, p 4; Richards, 2001, p 101) have also reported the difficulties they encountered in persuading family members to take part in their research studies. Arthur et al studied 31 families but were able to interview four family members in only four of these families. Such difficulties weaken the quality of research but were not considered to be a reason to avoid research of this kind.

The current study was able to explore the views of members of 44 different families. There was one family in which a child, both parents and both maternal and paternal grandparents were interviewed. There were seven families where it was possible to complete four interviews, 14 families in which three interviews took place, 18 with two interviews and four families in which it was possible to talk only to one parent (see Appendix, Table A2).

The structure of the book

This chapter and Chapter Two (which reviews all that we know about grandparenting) form an introduction to the book. Chapters Three to Six focus on the evidence about grandparenting and grandparents' relationships with their grandchildren. Chapter Seven is an introduction to grandparenting in divorced families and a preparation for discussion of some of the legal and family policy issues that are a particular focus of attention in the final chapters of this book. Chapters Eight to Eleven focus on post-divorce grandparenting and Chapter Twelve provides discussion of the main findings and the policy conclusions.

It is in the nature of this small-scale exploratory research that it raises questions that we are not always able to answer. Therefore, this study should be seen as a step towards uncovering more information about relationships between the generations in divorced families. Although grandparent research is a relatively new and rapidly expanding area of investigation, the current interest, we argue, is no passing fashion. It is a topic that is likely to remain of interest to researchers and policy makers for many years to come.

TWO

What do we already know about grandparents?

Researching grandparenting

Interest in grandparenting has increased considerably in recent years, particularly in Britain and the US. However, the quality of grandparent research has often been the subject of sharply critical comment. For example, Allen et al (2000) expressed concern about research that did not take account of "the total support network" (p 916). Studies which investigate the relationships between a grandparent and a favourite grandchild, or which ask college students to recount their childhood memories of their grandparents (Kornhaber and Woodward, 1981; Matthews and Sprey, 1984; Creasey and Koblewski, 1991), need to be treated cautiously since they do not fully recognise the importance of the part that parents, their children and other members of the wider family play in defining grandparents' roles.

Allen et al (2000) also criticised research that assumed that the nature of family relationships could be captured in a single snapshot, and thus placed reliance upon cross-sectional designs rather than longitudinal studies. Amato and Keith (1991) were critical of studies that did not ensure that "social class and other variables" were controlled (p 32). They urged researchers to avoid "relying on parents' ratings as their sole source of information" (p 33) and described convenience samples of volunteer subjects as "troubling" (p 31). Uhlenberg and Hammill (1998, p 276) commented on the fact that past research has not provided consistent findings about the variables that account for differences in grandparent behaviour. Szinovacz (1998, p 282) also criticised cross-sectional studies and the "prevalence of surveys and interviews" but seemed to approve of studies that were restricted to the study of grandparent–grandchild dyads. However, Aquilino's (1999) study of parent–child closeness, contact, control and conflict concluded that findings are significantly affected by whether or not the information is given by the first, the second or the third generation.

Studies that fail to comply with the logic of experiments risk the accusation that their findings have been built on shaky foundations. At the same time, although critics demand large representative samples and sophisticated measures, few of them mention the problems of persuading families to take part in the research (discussed in Chapter One of this book). Hetherington and Stanley-Hagan (1999, p 130) in their study of the effects of divorce on children's adjustment commented:

It is unfortunate, however, that the large sociological survey studies with representative samples usually have inadequate measures and often single informants, whereas the smaller psychological studies, which use more refined and sophisticated measures, continue to use non-representative samples of convenience.

Despite some telling criticisms from the research community, it can be argued that an accumulation of evidence from a host of imperfect studies in different styles has meant that some findings have been replicated often enough to convince all but the most demanding critics. In this chapter, we argue that research has progressed imperfectly but has now reached a stage in its development when it is important to ask new questions. These must go beyond the establishment of correlations between grandparent characteristics (age, gender, distance from grandchild's home, and so forth) and begin to look at the causes and effects of grandparenting behaviour. It seems important, from the outset, to establish what we know – or think we know – about grandparents and grandparenting.

Grandparents' support for their adult children and grandchildren

What has clearly emerged from research over the last two or three decades is the fact that grandparents are an important source of help, advice and support for parents and grandchildren. Grandparents' financial, emotional and childcare support for their families has been reported in numerous studies (Cherlin and Furstenberg, 1985; Kornhaber, 1996; Dench and Ogg, 2002). This support role is particularly important when parents separate and divorce. Tinsley and Parke (1984), Johnson (1985, 1998a, 1998b), and McLanahan and Booth (1989) have all commented on the vital role that is played by grandparents following the loss of a parent through divorce. Thompson (1999, p 471) suggested that grandparents "provide crucial help at all levels" and pointed out that they act "as practical everyday carers, as emotional anchors, firm but gentle childrearers, as models for achievement, as listeners and as transmitters of crucial information". Family breakdown creates a demand for support and, as our investigation discovered (see Chapter Ten), maternal grandparents who were involved in childcare when the parents were together will often experience an increase in their level of involvement.

Exchange Theory and reciprocity

Grandparents' support role is sometimes depicted as a series of transactions that are silently bargained or openly negotiated within a family group. It is a view that reminds us that social behaviour is motivated and that it is legitimate to ask who gets what from the deal. Finch (1989) asks whether kinship is a bargain struck by family members and whether "a balance sheet" (1989, p 166) of services and goods received is an appropriate analogy. This view is encapsulated in Exchange Theory (see Thibaut and Kelley, 1959; Homans, 1961; Chadwick-Jones, 1976). However, the evidence of dedicated grandparents suggests a different model of kinship. As we shall see in Chapter Ten, grandparents made sacrifices but had, it seemed, little prospect of seeing any return on their investment except the pleasure of knowing that they had supported their family. Arthur et al (2002, p 69) concluded that

> ... a simple 'moral economy' model that describes exchanges of help and support does not fully explain levels of grandmother satisfaction with their role. Grandmothers were strongly resistant to the idea of helping their grandchildren in order to receive help or support back in return.

Indeed, we might conclude that an overt exchange of goods or services would greatly diminish the benefit that grandparents derive from knowing that they had fulfilled their obligations. Grandparents, in this view, look after grandchildren because they love them and enjoy their company – not for any other reason and certainly not for financial reward.

Although Exchange Theory cannot provide a general explanation for grandparent support, our study, nevertheless, remained alert to the possibility of discovering particular circumstances in which exchanges seemed to apply. As we shall see, our study did uncover some examples of behaviour that seemed consistent with the notion of 'a kinship ledger' or the idea that it is important, on occasions, to consider the part that exchange and reciprocity might play.

Often, however, it is grandparents' altruism (Kornhaber, 1996) or strong sense of family obligation that explain their willingness to make sacrifices for the children and grandchildren. It seems safe to conclude that previous research has established that grandparents' have a deeply felt sense of obligation to their children and grandchildren which is the key to understanding their role as family supporters. Aldous (1995) drew attention to the powerful influence of 'the norm of obligation' but criticises what she perceives to be the attitude of government in the US to grandparent support. Aldous suggests that the norm of obligation has become an excuse for a neglect of other forms of support that is needed by the poorest families. She concludes that there may be "an assumption that aid from older generations, because of the obligation norm, will take care of these impoverished families" (1995, p 109). The findings of research into grandparents' support role seem to suggest that this assumption is well founded. However, the reasons why grandparents do or do not respond to requests to support the wider family is a question that would benefit from further investigation.

Distance from grandparents' home

Uhlenberg and Hammill (1998, p 276) have suggested that "A new study is not needed to establish that geographic distance is a strong predictor of frequency of intergenerational contact". In fact, every study that has used a measure of distance from grandparents' homes has come to the same conclusion: distance matters. Cherlin and Furstenberg (1992) concluded that distance had significant effects on the frequency of contact between grandparents and their grandchildren.

> If asked to name the three most important determinants of the frequency of contact between grandparents and grandchildren, we would have to reply 'distance, distance, distance'. (Cherlin and Furstenberg, 1992, p 117)

Matthews and Sprey (1984), Kivett (1991), Hodgson (1992) and Cooney and Smith (1996) have all noted that the number of miles between a grandchild's house and their grandparents' home was the most powerful predictor of 'grandparent–grandchild solidarity'. Boszormenghnagy and Spark (1973, p 218) pointed out, however, that geographic distance was not just the cause but also, on occasions, a symptom of emotional distance between grandparents and their adult children. Should this be correct, it could be concluded that not all grandparents who live a long way from their grandchildren's home do so by accident. Thompson (1999), drawing on evidence from French sociologists, noted that, although co-residence is rare in France, two in three parents with young children live close (that is, less than 20 km) to their own parents. Their study concluded that "living close is indeed related to feeling emotionally close" (1999, p 473).

These conclusions, however, may have been accepted too readily and may have been overstated. Our research (see Chapter Nine of this book) noted that a grandchild who rarely sees the paternal grandparents might continue to feel close to them. It would not be surprising to discover that there are exceptions to the findings about the relationship between geographical and emotional distance. Although distance predicts frequency of contact, it might not be closely related to the quality of the grandchild–grandparent relationship that can be maintained by exchanges of email, letters and telephone calls. Cherlin and Furstenberg (1992, p 117) have commented that geographical distance "makes the most difference in relationships that we feel obligated to maintain". They add, "the quality of that contact is another matter" (p 118). Such findings alert us to the dangers of tacitly assuming that the frequency of intergenerational contact is an indicator of the quality of relationships between grandparents and their children and grandchildren.

Parents' relationships with grandparents and the quality of grandparent–grandchild relationships

Research has established that the quality of parents' relationships with their own parents and parents-in-law determines the quality of their children's relationships with their grandparents (Johnson and Barer, 1987; Johnson, 1998b; Kivett, 1991; Hodgson, 1992). Grandparents, therefore, are said to have a 'mediated' (Gladstone, 1989, Drew and Smith, 1999) or 'derived' (Johnson, 1998a, p 188) relationship, in the sense that parents can facilitate or frustrate grandparents' attempts to maintain close relationships with their grandchildren. Werner (1991, p 74) has suggested that "The middle generation serves as a bridge between grandparent and grandchild". In her discussion of grandparenting in a divorced family, Johnson (1985, p 91) commented that grandparents' actions are "constrained by the mandate on the autonomy and privacy of the nuclear family in each generation and ultimately rest on the wishes of their children and children in law".

Werner (1991, p 74) has argued that a harmonious relationship between grandparents and parents, especially between mothers and grandmothers, provides the conditions in which grandparents' relationship with grandchildren can flourish. Johnson (1985), Cherlin and Furstenberg (1992) and Werner (1991) are among the authors who have argued that compatibility in the values of parents and grandparents is found when intergenerational ties are strong. Grandparents have to achieve a sometimes delicate balance between providing support for parents who need their help and observing parents' rights to determine how their children should be brought up. Grandparents are likely to want to avoid being seen as 'interfering' (by criticising parents' lifestyles, for example, or advising them on bringing up their children). There is, it seems, an underlying tension in which the onus is on the grandparents to comply with parents' wishes in matters of grandchildren's upbringing and socialisation. What research does not tell us is whether or not this tension is a significant factor in parent–grandparent relationships or an effect that has occasional repercussions for grandparenting behaviour. Dench and Ogg (2002, p 107) have considered this question and have commented that maternal grandmothers record high levels of agreement with the way that parents are bringing up children that do not diminish significantly when parents are apart. This suggests that, for maternal grandparents, major disagreements are rare. However, these authors describe paternal grandmothers' position as 'routinely delicate' and when parents have separated, their "levels of declared agreement drop substantially, and their 'say' virtually disappears" (Dench and Ogg, 2002, p 107). The view that grandparenting is a mediated or derived role needs to be qualified and refined.

The different roles of grandmothers and grandfathers

Researchers often assert that grandfathers and grandmothers interpret their roles in different ways. Should we be suspicious of claims about differences between grandmothers and grandfathers that seem to reflect a traditional view of men's and women's status within the family? Women, we are asked to believe, make the telephone calls, notice changes and pay compliments, remember birthdays, express affection more readily, check on others' well-being, oil the wheels of social discourse, attend to the family's needs and recognise when help and support is needed. Men, in this traditional view, play a supporting role and adopt a stance of being 'out of touch' and depending on their wives to keep them informed about the fine details of their grandchildren's lives. Women are the 'kin-keepers' (Troll, 1985; Spitze and Ward, 1998; Roberto, et al, 2001) and are more likely at every age to be close to their children and grandchildren. Grandmothers anticipate grandparenthood earlier, become involved in their grandparenting role sooner than grandfathers (Creasey and Koblewski, 1991) and embrace the role with greater enthusiasm than grandfathers. They are more likely to become key figures in their young grandchildren's lives and interpret the task in distinctively different ways (Aldous, 1985; Hagestad, 1985; Troll, 1985; Eisenberg, 1988; Mills et al, 2001).

Men, it is often claimed, are less involved in the day-to-day activities of family life while women are the 'glue' that holds family and kinship together and have the "primary responsibility for holding kin groups together" (Dubas, 2001, p 480). Research on fatherhood (Burghes et al, 1997) demonstrates that men spend relatively little time on a one-to-one-basis with their children. It has been suggested that fathers have to 'catch up' with their children at weekends (O'Brien and Jones, 1996) and engage mainly in leisure activities rather than 'childcare' when they are sharing their sons' and daughters' company. Allen et al (2000), commenting on Cooney and Uhlenberg's (1990) research, suggest that the lack of connection that many divorced men feel with their adult children has only recently been recognised. However, Burghes et al (1997, p 63) warned their readers that there was too little reliable quantitative data to make firm judgements about changes that might or might not have taken place in recent years in men's attitudes to family relationships. Roberto et al (2001) were just as reluctant to confirm that grandparents fit the traditional gender stereotypes and drew attention to the fact that most of what is known about grandparents is based on women's experience of grandparenting:

> Given traditional gender roles and the prevalence of 'kin-keeping', among women, it is not surprising that there is a gender bias in the grandparenting literature. (Roberto et al, 2001, p 409)

Despite these doubts about gender stereotyping, there is no equivalent body of evidence to suggest that grandfathers are as active as grandmothers in 'kin-keeping', or as interested in their grandparenting role. However, King and Elder (1997, p 850) have commented: "Studies that examine gender differences on a variety of measures often find that grandmothers and grandfathers show more similarities than differences". There is, however, a lack of research that has set out to consider grandfathers separately and discover why they seem to be restricted to a secondary role. Roberto et al (2001, p 408) comment that "there is a gender gap in the literature" and suggest that "most of what is known about grandparents is based on the perceptions of older women".

Grandparent discipline

Research on grandparent discipline is sparse and provides a confusing picture. Smith (1991) notes that Gesell and Ilg (1946) – influential American developmental psychologists – drew attention to the "numerous hazards of grandparent interference with parental control" (Smith, 1991, p 3). He also quotes Vollmer (1937), who held similarly negative views. Thompson (1952) claimed that conflicts frequently arose as a result of the differing child-rearing practices of parents and grandparents. Kornhaber (1996, p 29), who also quoted the findings of studies from around the period of the Second World War, comments on the differences between the relatively positive views of grandparents in contemporary research and the harsh verdicts of earlier studies. Kornhaber explains that the experts in child development of half a century ago had backgrounds in psychotherapy and their opinions had been formed as a result of their experience of working with dysfunctional grandparents in families that were not typical of the wider population. Smith (1991) suggests that changes in image fuelled by children's literature and changing fashions had the effect of providing grandparents with 'a bad press' that influenced the perceptions of grandparenting throughout the society of the period. Grandparent discipline is discussed in Chapter Five of this book.

The number of grandchildren

The grandparents in our study included one maternal grandmother who had seven children from her first marriage and 20 grandchildren. Her husband had four grandchildren from his first marriage. She was able to see all of her grandchildren and step-grandchildren regularly and, on occasions, sets of grandchildren from different families would call at the house at the same time. She was able to list all of their names but encountered some difficulties in doing so. It appears self-evident that the emotional investment of a grandmother with 20 or more grandchildren in any one of her grandchildren is likely to be proportionately less than that of a grandmother who is close to her only grandchild. Our study did not investigate the relationship between the number of grandchildren and the quality of grandparents' relationships. However, Uhlenberg and Hammill (1998, p 283) did study this question and concluded:

> As the number of sets increases, the likelihood of frequent contact with any particular set decreases and the likelihood of infrequent contact increases. Nevertheless, the probability of having frequent contact with at least one set of grandchildren is greater for grandparents with multiple sets than those with only one set.

This is an example of grandparents' selective investment in grandchildren (Cherlin and Furstenberg, 1985) which is further discussed in Chapter Ten.

Grandparent and resident parent employment

Grandparents with busy working lives might be expected to have fewer opportunities to share their grandchildren's company. Like grandparents who have a number of grandchild sets and those who live far away from their grandchildren, their opportunities for contact may be more restricted than those of grandparent couples in which one or both grandparents are retired or unemployed. Grandparents who are working, however, may feel better able to provide financial assistance.

Dench and Ogg (2002, p 95) have commented that "as the effects of new career patterns work their way through the family cycle, the support given by grandparents may increasingly take *either* financial or practical forms". However, these authors also described a minority of 'supergrans' who not only worked and provided financial help but who also helped in a substantial way to care for their grandchildren. When mothers are employed, grandparents who are providing childcare are likely to feel more dissatisfied than those who are making financial sacrifices or who are providing only occasional support for resident parents. Dench and Ogg (2002, p 98) have commented that it is not the pressure on grandmothers to provide childcare for working mothers that is new but their resistance to it. Most of the grandparents in our study were aged 60+ and few were still in paid employment. However, there were examples of retired grandparents whose divorced daughters were in full-time employment who had considerable childcare responsibilities and they became a focus for attention in this study (see Chapter Ten of this book).

Maternal and paternal grandparents

The existence of a 'grandparenting hierarchy' has been identified in a number of research studies. Findler (2000), for example, compared the support role of grandparents with disabled and non-disabled grandchildren. Grandmothers on both sides of the family and maternal grandfathers were ranked among the eight most important support providers in the disability group and among the first six in the control group. In both groups, the maternal grandmother was frequently ranked first ahead of her husband. Findler concluded that this hierarchy indicated the central role of maternal grandparents and of the maternal grandmother in particular. It is a finding that may require some further elaboration and interpretation. We have found the concept of a principal grandparent helpful, and this is discussed in Chapter Six of this book. Aldous (1995) and Johnson (1998b, p 188) confirm that gender and lineage often act to produce a hierarchy with maternal grandmothers at the top and paternal grandfathers at the bottom. Johnson (1998b) explains that 'the matrifocal bias' or female linkages strengthen after a divorce, and quotes Rossi and Rossi's (1990) view that separated and divorced mothers have a greater developmental stake in preserving and strengthening their ties to their parents.

Paternal grandmothers, in both intact and divorced families, may be seen as competitors with maternal grandparents and might be excluded from contact with their grandchildren (Dench and Ogg, 2002, p 60). And when parents part, fathers may not be able to provide contact for their own parents (Johnson, 1998b, p 189). Cherlin and Furstenberg (1992) and Douglas and Lowe (1990) have also noted that, when a marriage breaks down, maternal grandparents become more active in their role while some paternal grandparents may find themselves excluded from having contact with their grandchildren. Leek and Smith (1991) make the point that, in intact families, mothers are more frequently at home during the day and grandparents feel more comfortable visiting their own daughter than their daughter-in-law. Because grandparenting, as we noted earlier, is 'mediated' by parents, it is therefore likely that grandchildren will be closer to their grandparents on the mother's side of the family. The differences between maternal and paternal grandparents' roles and functions are discussed in greater detail in Chapter Six.

Grandparents' marital status

Grandparents' marital status is believed to have a significant effect on the frequency of contact with grandchildren. Uhlenberg and Hammill (1998), for example, noted that married grandparents are most likely to maintain frequent contact with their grandchildren followed by widowed, remarried and divorced grandparents. Their finding that unmarried grandfathers are much less likely to maintain contact reinforces the view that women are more active in maintaining family relationships. Ferri and Smith's (1996) study identifies a group of 'highly involved fathers' who made up only a third of their sample. The study found that the 11% of mothers with uninvolved husbands were vulnerable to emotional disorder. Its authors commented that,

> By contrast fathers' marital happiness, overall life satisfaction and emotional state were only tenuously linked to their level of involvement with their children. (Ferri and Smith, 1996, p 49)

Should the same be true of grandfathers, the Uhlenberg and Hammill (1998) finding might be explained by the fact that widowed and divorced grandfathers in particular have lost the impetus in family matters that their wives might otherwise have provided. Their study controlled for differences in grandparent age, so it is unlikely that age differences between single and married grandparents could account for the finding. Our study comments briefly on relationships between older grandchildren and their widowed maternal grandmothers (see Chapter Eight); however, we were unable to undertake an analysis of the relationship between grandparents' marital status and the closeness of the grandparent–grandchild relationship. In fact, few researchers have systematically studied this, and Kornhaber (1996, p 123) commented that little research has been done on the effects of grandparents' remarriage on relationships with grandchildren.

Race and ethnicity

In Chapter One, we explained that no Asian or African Caribbean parents accepted our invitation to take part in the research. Studies in Britain have not yet given much prominence to grandparents from Asian and African Caribbean communities (but see Richards, 2001). However, there has been research on black and minority ethnic grandparents in the US. Cherlin and Furstenberg (1992) found substantial differences in the US between black and white grandparents' behaviour. They noted that African-American grandparents exhibited more 'parent-like' behaviour (1992, p 127) and provided, on average, significantly more discipline and general childcare than American grandparents of European descent. In this study, 40% of black grandparents (but only 18% of white grandparents) reported that they had lived with their grandchildren for a period of three months or more. Gibson (2002), in a study of 12 African-American grandmothers with full-time care of their grandchildren, concluded that their view of themselves as the only viable source of help and their strongly held cultural and religious beliefs helped to explain their willingness to accept responsibility for grandchildren. Strom et al (1993) commented on differences between the grandparenting of African-American and white grandparents, while McCready (1985) found differences between ethnic groups in the US and claimed that those of Scandinavian origin, for example, were more distant in their relationship with their grandchildren than grandparents of Polish origin. Hurme (1991) made a similar comment about the quality of the grandparenting of Finnish grandparents.

The general message from research on race is that African-American grandparents accept more responsibility for the day-to-day care of their grandchildren. More live with grandchildren in tri-generational households, more have become their grandchildren's full-time carers and more share care of children with parents. In the UK, Richards (2001) noted that grandparents from minority ethnic groups emphasised the importance of handing down cultural and religious traditions to their grandchildren and were willing to accept major childcare responsibilities. What is not clear in some of the American research and in Richard's study of minority ethnic families, however, is how much of the difference can be attributed to the values, beliefs and traditions of minority ethnic groups and how much might be true of poor communities in all cultures.

Age of grandparents and their grandchildren

Silverstein and Long's (1998) longitudinal study discovered that grandparents' contact with their grandchildren varied with age and that older grandchildren saw their grandparents less frequently. The age of the grandchild (Matthews and Sprey, 1985) and the age of the grandparent (Burton and Bengtson, 1985; Somary and Stricker, 1998) helped to account for the frequency of grandchild–grandparent contact. Adolescent grandchildren saw their grandparents less frequently than younger grandchildren. When groups of grandparents in different age ranges were compared, it was found that older grandparents had less contact with their grandchildren than younger grandparents. While research may have established correlations between frequency and quality of contact and grandparents' and grandchildren's age, it does not tell us about the exceptions or the circumstances in which relationships between older grandparents and their grandchildren might continue undiminished. It is not certain whether age and the quality of the relationship are related in linear fashion or whether there are peaks (perhaps in early childhood and adulthood) and troughs in adolescence. It is possible, too, that the relationships between grandparent age and the quality of relationships with grandchildren might be largely accountable in terms of variation in grandparent health or the incidence of full- and part-time employment. The effects of grandchild and grandparent age on relationships are explored in Chapter Three.

Styles of grandparenting

Some studies have attempted a description and classification of 'grandparent styles'. Cherlin and Furstenberg (1985) described, in turn, 'detached', 'passive', 'supportive', 'authoritative' and 'influential' grandparents. They noted in their nationally representative sample that most black grandparents (1985, p 104) were 'authoritative' or 'influential', while few were classified as 'passive'. In their book, *The new American grandparent* (Cherlin and Furstenberg, 1992), they changed their classifications to 'remote', 'companionate' and 'involved'. These latter categories were a reflection of the amount of contact with grandchildren – with the distinction between 'companionate' and 'involved' grandparenting depending largely on perceptions of the degree to which grandparents exhibited 'parent-like' behaviour. Neugarten and Weinstein (1964) suggested a classification of characteristic grandparenting roles that is frequently cited in more recent studies. They suggested that grandparents could be classified into five types: 'formal', 'fun-seeker', 'distant figure', 'surrogate parent' and 'reservoir of family wisdom'. Mueller et al (2002) largely confirmed the findings of previous research by suggesting five grandparent styles: 'influential', 'supportive', 'passive', 'authority-oriented' and 'detached'. Whether a particular grandparent can fit into more than one of these roles (or even all at once), switch from role to role depending on the context, or adopt different styles with different grandchildren, is not made entirely clear. 'Funseeking' grandparents are discussed in this study, but it also suggests some new dimensions of grandparenting in a divorced family that might benefit from further investigation (see Chapter Twelve).

Concluding comments

If it is possible for the results of investigations to seem simultaneously prosaic and controversial, then grandparent studies might seem to have achieved this distinction. As we have seen, a considerable body of research has aimed to account for variations in grandparents' perceptions of their roles, their emotional attachment to their grandchildren and the frequency of their contact with grandchildren. Much of the early research attempted to make predictions from the gender, race, age and social class variables that are the familiar grist to the social scientist's research mill. The discovery of a link between geographical distance and frequency of contact is hardly surprising. Nor should there be surprise that "the grandparent role has many sides to it", that "aspects of the role vary according to different factors" or that grandparenting "is not a uniform phenomenon" (Hurme, 1991, pp 19, 23). There are certainly gaps in our knowledge and it appears that some of the most interesting questions are the most difficult to answer.

The study of grandparents, however, reflects perhaps a pattern of progress that is quite common in social science. The first phase has surveyed the landscape and identified significant differences between the characteristics or behaviour of groups of grandparents that differ in age, ethnic origin, social class and so forth. The second phase is underway, as attempts are being made to explore and refine some of the relationships and differences that earlier research has identified. The next phase will be to identify new questions that might be investigated with systematic, longitudinal studies. These studies will be faced with the challenge of applying sophisticated measures to large, representative samples of family members who can provide a cross-generational perspective.

Our study has looked at grandparent and grandchild age, the differences between grandmothers and grandfathers, paternal and maternal grandparenting, grandparent support and other topics that have been the subject of previous research. Our aim, however, was not to replicate previous findings but to explore the dynamics of the grandparent–grandchild relationship and the impact of parental divorce on grandparents' relationships with their families. Our hope is that the findings that will be described in the remainder of this book will generate ideas about aspects of grandparents' roles that will benefit from further investigation.

THREE

Grandparents' relationships with grandchildren: continuity and change

A changing relationship

In Chapter Two, we discussed some of the factors that previous studies have indicated influence the nature of grandparents' relationships with their grandchildren. In this chapter, we ask: 'What importance do grandchildren attach to their relationship with their grandparents and how might these relationships be affected by divorce? And, 'is there evidence of continuity in the grandparent–grandchild relationship in divorced families as well as evidence of change as the result of family break-up?'.

Grandparent's relationships with their grandchildren

The studies reviewed in Chapter Two made it clear that grandparent age is related to the frequency of grandparents' contact with their grandchildren and that older grandchildren have less contact with their grandparents. But does this mean that they are not as emotionally close to their grandparents? Here, we begin by considering the views of some teenage grandchildren and their feelings about their grandparents. They reported that they have close relationships with their grandparents, but this assertion was often accompanied by apparently contradictory evidence of a growing emotional distance. Being 'close to grandparents' could mean seeing them regularly, enjoying their company, sharing intimacies and expressing affection. However, we discovered that the phrase need not imply anything about frequency of contact and was used on occasion to mean 'nurturing positive feelings'. Evidence from divorced parents suggested that older grandchildren saw their grandparents less frequently than their younger brothers and sisters. Mothers, we discovered, occasionally reminded their children that they had not seen their grandparents for some time and persuaded them to accompany them on a visit to their grandparents' home. They reported a gradual reduction in their children's contact with their grandparents. Most felt that this did not mean that relationships could no longer be described as 'close' or that grandchildren and grandparents felt less affection for each other. It was, in parents' opinions, understandable that the relationship should change.

Alfie's mother had been separated for two years before her decree nisi was granted over four years ago. She had a particularly close relationship with her parents who lived about a mile away and had been very supportive of her and her three children, aged 12, 16 and 18. She commented that the maternal grandparents' 'unconditional love' had taught her a lot about bringing up her own children. She was one of the many parents who remarked that the children had reduced the frequency of their contact with their grandparents but emphasised that this did not mean that their affection for them had diminished.

The thing is, their ages are different now. They were little toddlers then – when they were tiny, you know. I would say they still have a good relationship with them [their maternal grandparents]. It's just a different relationship. It's more of a 'Let's catch up on your news. What's happening in your life?'.

Alfie (aged 12) confirmed that he liked to see his maternal grandparents and went on to describe his contact with them:

They come here and they go in the front room for the afternoon. It's usually on a Wednesday. I think they come here about quarter past one usually and speak to my mum. They leave about five [o'clock]. They go home for their tea. I sometimes go down their house as well, just for no reason, really. Sometimes I help them with their PC as well.

Alfie's maternal grandfather, however, had complained to his daughter that he and his wife saw very little of their two older grandchildren. Alfie's mother commented:

My dad has questioned why they haven't popped down. C [Alfie's sister] won't think 'Oh, I'll pop down and visit nan and pamps tonight'. She's a busy bee. J [Alfie's brother], no, he won't. He is far too busy. He has a little job after school a few nights a week and he's got his GCSEs at the moment. I might say to Alfie, 'I'm popping down mum and dad's. Do you want to come down?', 'Yeah', he would say, 'I haven't seen them for a while, I'll come down'.

The mother's description of her 16-year-old son's infrequent meetings with his maternal grandmother provided a good example of a grandmother's love for her grandson and his response to her exuberant expressions of affection.

J [Alfie's older brother] is the quiet one and he is a lovely young man and when my mum sees him, she goes, 'Oh, here he is! Oh, I love this boy!'. And she is really huggy with J.

He goes, 'Oh, Nanny!'. She goes, 'You won't take me to bingo when I'm old and grey!' and he goes, 'I would!'. And he would!

In another family, Tom was eight years old and his brother was five. They spent alternate weekends with their father. Tom's father said that his relationship with his parents was not a close one and, although they had given him a lot of support at the time of his divorce, he felt that this had not brought them closer together. Tom and his brother saw their paternal grandparents during their weekends with their father and the two boys greatly enjoyed these visits to their grandparents' home. Tom's father was aware that grandparent–grandchild relationships change over time and seemed to be anticipating a change in his sons' relationships with their paternal grandparents.

> The kids would tell me if they didn't like it [going to their paternal grandparents' house] but they're still at a young age where they go along with the flow. Give it three more years and Tom might suddenly say, 'I don't want to go nan's. I want to play with little Johnny down the road'.

Some mothers also believed that their older children saw less of their maternal grandparents because they had begun to concentrate their attention increasingly on their peer group, as well as their schoolwork and a wider range of activities that took them away from the family. William's mother noted that there was a danger that her older children's changed relationships with their maternal and paternal grandparents might wrongly be attributed to her divorce.

> There was a spell when they saw more of them after we'd split up. But they were younger then and now they're in their later teens. No children see their grandparents as much [when they are in their teens]. They do see them but not as much. Now they've got their own lives, they're different children than they were six years ago [at the time of the parents' separation]. So I don't think it would have been any different had we all been together.

One father reported that his adolescent daughters' 'obsession' with horse riding explained why they saw so little of their grandparents and a mother suggested that her daughter's interest in dancing was the explanation. Some adolescent grandchildren confirmed that they rarely saw their grandparents even though they lived near their grandparents' home and the interviews with grandparents suggested that they were well aware that their grandchildren had apparently distanced themselves from the relationship.

> Alan's grandmother suggested that she could "do things with them when they were smaller" but "as they grow up with friends and dates and things" the relationship changed. She added, "He is so often out when I go there. He plays rugby and he is out with his friends". Alan was now 16 and lived with his mother, her new husband and his son and his sister who was away at university. The maternal grandmother lived 25 miles away from Alan's home and was visited regularly by her daughter. Alan rarely accompanied his mother on these visits and his grandmother could not disguise her disappointment or

> her concern that her grandchild's 'family duties' might be a burden to him. She worried that Alan's mother may have had to persuade him to accompany her and that his occasional visits were rooted in 'family obligation' rather than affection.
>
> I say to him that it's a shame that he has to come here, on a nice day when he could be at the beach or doing something else because he is such an outdoor person.
>
> Alan felt that he had a good relationship with his grandmother, and while he recognised that he saw her infrequently, he did not think that this meant that his relationship with her was not a close one.
>
> Well, I think I'm quite close, it's just that time is really – I just don't have enough time.
>
> He went on to explain that his sporting commitments, his schoolwork and the time spent seeing his father, kept him busy.

Grandparents usually understood why older grandchildren seemed less interested in them and most accepted the inevitability of their situation. Children with divorced parents spend time with their non-resident parents and it may be that this curtails other activities, including visits to grandparents and time spent with friends. It is also possible that grandchildren did not want to admit that their grandparents were no longer significant figures in their lives. They may have preferred to make socially acceptable statements and confirm the popular image of grandparents as close and loving members of the wider family. Grandchildren may not have disentangled their feelings from 'the family view' and, in the words of the father quoted above, are happy to 'go with the flow' until they reach an age when they decide for themselves that there are more interesting things to do. The fact that some adolescent children did not find time in their busy lives for their grandparents did not necessarily contradict their view that they, nevertheless, felt emotionally close.

It might be argued, however, that grandparents value the grandparent–grandchild relationship more highly than their adolescent grandchildren. Finch (1989) has commented that the relationship is 'not symmetrical' in the sense that grandchildren's feelings of affection for their grandparents are not reciprocated to the same extent by their grandchildren. The interviews with grandchildren that were conducted in this study led us to the conclusion that Finch was right to suggest that relationships between adolescent grandchildren and their grandparents are often rather one-sided or 'asymmetrical'.

Older grandparents

The age of the grandparents (see Chapter Two) is also thought to be an important influence on the quality of the grandchild–grandparent relationship. However, Roberto et al (2001) point out that older grandparents in their study, with good mental and physical health, continued to play a more active role in their grandchildren's lives.

In our interviews, grandparents mentioned poor health in particular as a restricting factor and this leads us to suspect that health measures might prove to be more powerful predictors of the quality of grandparents' relationships than a simple age measure. For example, Tony's mother realised that her parents' enthusiasm for grandparenting had waned.

> I wouldn't say that they have this really fantastic 'lovey' relationship, because they haven't really. I think that she [maternal grandmother] did more with my older boys because she wasn't so worn out then. She had them when they were really tiny and she was younger then and had more energy I suppose. She has done it for years really.

Other parents in our study noted that older grandparents were not as actively involved with grandchildren and some felt grandparents' values and outlook were as important as physical factors. Some parents perceived the grandparents to be old-fashioned, out of touch with children's needs and disapproving of the new generation. Pat's father provided an example of a fairly common view of this perception of difference between older and younger grandparents.

> He [Pat's step-maternal grandfather] is a lot younger than my mother and father. He's a very active 60. He's like a 50-year-old, not a 60-year-old. Pat knows she can't do that with our mum and dad [paternal grandparents in their seventies]. But dad can't go very far and mum's got breathing problems, and they're limited in what they can do. Also, mum and dad are very old-fashioned. What Pat would like to do on a day out, I don't think they'd think much of it.

George's mother also believed that her parents had been left behind by the changes that have taken place in contemporary family life.

> My dad gets cross with them sometimes. I don't know that he realises that teenagers now are a little bit different than they were when we were all younger.

Karen's maternal grandmother lived some distance away from her grandchildren (a three-hour car journey) and saw them only once or twice each year. However, she was among those grandparents who were willing to admit that they did not much enjoy their grandchildren's company.

> I think part of the problem is that children are brought up differently now, you see, and of course you tend, as you get older, you tend to get a bit set about this and sometimes you don't really agree with the way things are done in someone else's family. Obviously, I wouldn't dream of saying anything, you know and obviously when the parents are there it's up to them, but I get a bit irritated, I must admit. Much as I love them, I do get a bit irritated because of their ways.

Pat's paternal grandfather agreed with these sentiments.

> Well, we're two different age groups, aren't we, eh? There isn't much you could talk to an 11-year-old about today really.

Grandparents' reservations about their relationships with grandchildren

Irene's maternal grandfather expressed his obligations to his grandchildren in a way that suggested that he preferred to be seen as an 'emergencies-only' or 'standby' grandparent. He felt that grandparents in divorced families should be ready to answer the call but, in the interview, he made it clear that he hoped that he would not be needed. His daughter (who herself had four daughters) commented:

> He was strange with me when I was a child. He couldn't cope with the noise that children make. He can't cope with it now. If they come in and they come in noisy, he has to go upstairs. So, when I was a child and I had friends around, he couldn't cope with it so he used to have to either send me out or go out of the way himself.

It was clear that reluctant grandparenting, as in this case, was neither an outcome of divorce nor a desire in later life to give a higher priority to other things. It was a continuation of attitudes and practices that had earlier origins.

Karen's grandparents, who described themselves as feeling 'irritated' by their grandchildren, were another example of 'reluctant' grandparenting in a couple who, it seemed, were not good with children and did not enjoy their company. Karen's mother had four children including one with significant learning difficulties and one who was autistic. She suffered from severe financial hardship and was afraid of her ex-husband who lived nearby, and suffered from depression. She was anxious to return to the town where she had been brought up so that she could receive help from her parents. The grandparents did not mention their daughter's desire to move nearer to them so could not be asked about it directly but when asked how they saw their daughter's future, they replied that they could not foresee any change. They had grandchildren in an intact family whom they saw once a week when their daughter-in-law brought them to the house. Both said that grandparenting was not an important part of their lives.

> I don't look upon it as a terribly important thing, I'll be quite honest with you. We've done the children bit, if you see what I mean. We've done that for many, many years, but I quite like having them, you know, just for a little while and then they can go off back to their parents sort of thing. It's very wearing. (Karen's maternal grandfather)

> I try very hard, but after a while of that, I am absolutely shattered. (Karen's maternal grandmother)

Linda (aged 10) explained that she did not visit her paternal grandparents who lived nearby and were still seeing her younger brother. She reported that her paternal grandmother had falsely accused her of stealing.

> I don't like going down one of my other nan's. Well, it is like I can't breathe down there.

As far as Linda was concerned, her relationship with these grandparents was at an end. Linda's mother revealed that her parents-in-law had been reluctant grandparents since her daughter's birth.

> Then Linda came along and I was told that they were too young to be grandparents and that they wanted to be known as Terry and Jean and not nan and granddad, grampy, grandma, whatever. And I mean they didn't take my feelings into account or anything. And my husband then, he just went along with whatever mummy and daddy said.

Neugarten and Weinstein's (1964) research in the US suggested that a third of all grandparents were dissatisfied with their role. In their study, some grandparents felt that grandparenting undermined their 'youthful image'. More recent research, however, does not support Neurgarten and Weinstein's views (see Kornhaber, 1996), and this mother's comment about her ex parents-in-law was the only suggestion of this kind that we discovered in our interviews with members of 44 divorced families. These particular grandparents were not willing to be interviewed but, if Linda's mother's comments were accurate, they appear to provide further confirmation that less close relationships with grandchildren often have their roots in long-standing attitudes rather than the effects of divorce.

The relationship between pre- and post-divorce grandparenting

Grandparents who did not have close relationships with their grandchildren were not always victims of changed relationships within the family after a divorce. A variety of reasons might be given by grandparents and parents for unenthusiastic grandparenting, but they usually included a reluctance to see grandparenting as a significant role. Negative attitudes to grandparenting, or simply a decision to give grandparenting a lower priority than other aspects of grandparents' lives, usually had origins that predated parents' separation and divorce. Parents did not say that the maternal and paternal grandparents had changed, but claimed rather that the reservations of some grandparents about their grandparenting role had been apparent during the years of their marriage.

Some who reflected on their own childhood suggested that their parents were not good with children and never had been. It is important, therefore, to note the continuities rather than focus on changes that might otherwise be seen as outcomes of divorce.

Valerie's mother was disappointed that her own mother was not a loving grandparent. However, when she was asked to think about her own childhood, it was clear that her ambivalent feelings had a long history.

> I'd love a relationship with my mum and I'd love her to be more involved with all the children and their lives and to be really, really interested. Without a question of doubt she loves us and she's got our interests at heart but she can't give more. It's taken me years to actually understand that because as a child I used to hit my head against a brick wall, not understanding it, wanting this affection. And I couldn't understand why I couldn't get it.

Robin's father, who was the resident parent, was critical of his mother who lived nearby but who had little interest in being a grandmother:

> I think she could make a bit more of an effort with the children. Even if it was only once a month, to take the children to the park or something wouldn't hurt.
>
> *Has her relationship changed since you split up?*
>
> No, she has always been like this.

Later in the interview he noted that his mother had other interests in her life.

> She is not interested in looking after the children but she runs a jazz club, a bowling society, she goes bowling and on holiday, but then she says that she can't come down and look after the children.

Eleanor's mother was disappointed that the paternal grandparents seemed to have lost interest in their grandchildren and believed that she could see an even longer history of poor parenting and grandparenting stretching back over two generations

> There was no natural enthusiasm to find out how they [the grandchildren] were developing, what they were doing, how they were, unless a phone call or a visit was made by us [the couple when they were still married]. It was the same with Eleanor's great grandparents. We [mother and children] only actually have anything to do with them if we're in touch with them. That was the same when we were married.

Although we found evidence to indicate that parents and their parents-in-law might sever previously close relationships with each other (see Chapter Nine), there was no equivalent body of evidence to suggest that close and loving grandparents decided to sever the relationship with their grandchildren. Those who had appeared to do so had, in fact, a history of what was perceived to be reluctant grandparenting.

Confiding in grandparents

A possible impact of parental divorce is to bring grandparents and their grandchildren closer together. We wondered whether grandchildren might turn to their grandparents for advice, share confidences and seek reassurance. However, we discovered that grandchildren did not usually want to discuss their parents' separation with their grandparents. Nine of the 30 grandchildren in our study reported that they either talked to their *maternal* grandparent or recalled that their maternal grandparents had spoken to them about family break-up. Few of them seemed to ask questions or seek advice but it was not always possible to be certain how the conversations that did take place had begun. Grandchildren themselves were not clear whether they had confided in their grandparents and some seemed to find the question difficult to answer. Almost half the grandchildren replied that they did not know or could not remember whether they had discussed their parents' separation or were quite certain that they had not discussed it with anyone at all. Only one of the 30 grandchildren (Ingrid) reported that she had shared confidences with a *paternal* grandparent. This finding is consistent with paternal grandparents' reports that they were less likely to have 'serious conversations' with their grandchildren (see Chapter Four of this book).

Although Ingrid had spoken to her paternal grandparents about her parents' separation, she had spoken much more to her maternal grandparents. Her mother and maternal grandparents had held informal 'group sessions' with Ingrid and her younger brother and sister. The sessions were wholly devoted to the discussion of 'family matters' and Ingrid's mother said that her children enjoyed the discussions and had all contributed enthusiastically to a range of topics including discussion of their parents' separation and divorce. This strategy may have contributed to a degree of openness that proved to be unusual among the members of the families that took part in this study.

We have what's called 'family chats' and my parents do it with them and I do it with them and the children like nothing better than sitting down round the table and we'll talk about things. We talk about school, we talk about friends, we talk about plans and we talk about family. And they do that with my parents. In fact my parents started that off during a holiday they took them on soon after the divorce. They spent every evening in a villa having 'a family chat'. (Ingrid's mother)

Those children who had discussed the break-up of their family with other people were most likely to mention that they had confided in their mother but some had talked to other family members as well. These included brothers and sisters as well as maternal grandparents. Douglas et al (2000) observed in their study that parents were a main source of emotional support for children in divorced families. Although Dunn and Deater-Deckard (2001) concluded that grandparents were key confidants for children, their evidence demonstrated that only a minority of grandchildren in their sample confided in their grandparents about family break-up. In a study by Dunn et al (2001), 62 children were asked whom they had confided in at the time of their parents' separation. The authors classified the responses into 'minor confiding' and 'intimate confiding' and noted that for intimate confiding, 'grandparents and other family members' – that is, not parents and siblings – was the largest category. However, this study demonstrated that only 14% of the sample confided in grandparents (see Dunn et al, 2001, p 278, fig 1). Dunn et al also noted that almost one in four children did not talk to anyone about their parents' separation.

In our study, every grandchild was asked directly whether he or she had talked to the maternal and paternal grandparents about family break-up. When Steve (aged 14) was asked why he confided in his maternal grandmother about his problems at school but had not talked to her about his parents' separation, he replied, "Because that is about school and the other would be more private". This could well be the result of children's desire to avoid situations in which their loyalty to one or other of their parents would be tested, but further research would be needed to investigate this hypothesis. Such research would need to be careful to define what it meant by the phrases 'sharing confidences' and providing 'emotional support'. Grandparents may well have said things to grandchildren that were intended to provide reassurance – 'Your mum and dad don't want to live together any more but they both still love you very much and they always will' – but grandchildren may or may not have viewed this as emotional support. The interviews indicated that few grandchildren initiated conversations about their parents' separation or took the opportunities that were given to them to explain their worries or ask their grandparents to help them to understand the implications of family break-up.

When Irene was asked whether she had confided in her grandparents when she felt worried about her parents' divorce, she made it clear that she had not. She was also asked whether she had wanted to ask them questions about her parents' decision to separate, but the answer was the same. She felt that her grandparents would have been helpful had she confided in them, but this was an 'unspoken understanding', rather than something that they had made explicit. Irene's grandparents had not attempted to talk to her about her parents' separation and she had not wanted them to do so.

Did you want to ask them [your grandparents] any questions?

No, I just sort of like wanted to stay out of it as much as I could. ...They never talked about mum and dad splitting up because they wouldn't say anything in front of us. I never asked them anything about the split. My grandparents never mentioned it but probably thought that if I did need to that I would have gone to them and asked. (Irene, aged 13)

Kate (aged 9) had not wanted to talk to her grandparents either and had received alot of reassurance from her mother. Although her reply is a rather strange one, she clearly felt that a parent rather than a grandparent was the right person to confide in.

Would your grandparents not be helpful in explaining things?

I don't know. Mummy was a child and I think she may understand my problems more.

Concluding comments

In the early stages of this study, it was thought that parental divorce would provide a new role for grandparents because they would become more involved in childcare and grandchildren would turn to them for emotional support. However, the interview transcripts contained no clear body of evidence to confirm this. Findings about the effects of parental divorce on the emotional bond between grandchildren and grandparents need to be accepted with some important reservations. We discovered that grandparents, who were reluctant to get involved with their grandchildren before the divorce, did not become more enthusiastic about grandparenting when the parents separated. The nature of the grandparent–grandchild relationship *before* the break-up of the family is, on this evidence, an important predictor of the post-divorce relationship.

The interview data left little room to doubt that children's growing independence from family control and influence meant that their relationships with their grandparents changed with the passing of time. Parents, grandchildren and grandparents themselves noted differences in the attitudes and behaviour of older and younger grandparents. Some grandparenting, as we have seen, is disadvantaged by grandparents' old age and physical frailty; but in other cases, it is their 'old-fashioned' attitudes and their intolerance that has hampered the development of better relationships. However, the changes that occurred as grandchildren and their grandparents grew older are difficult to disentangle from the longer-term impact of parental divorce. Our tentative conclusion is that the evidence of changes in pre- and post-divorce grandparenting is less compelling than the evidence of continuities.

While this evidence about continuities and the effects of grandchild–

grandparent age on the relationship should be seen as one of the major findings, there are other observations that should also be carried forward. Older grandchildren explained that their diminishing contact with their grandparents did not imply any loss of affection. During adolescence, relationships with peers and activities outside the home become increasingly important, but we do not assume that adolescents' attempts to assert their independence should necessarily be interpreted as a loss of love for parents. However, evidence of distance between grandchildren and their grandparents that increases with age does lend support to the view that the relationship is often 'asymmetrical' (see Finch, 1989). Grandparents who are permanently separated from their grandchildren may become distressed and suffer 'bereavement' (see Drew and Smith, 2002, p 115; Chapter Eleven of this book) and some may decide to seek a remedy in law. It is not apparent that grandchildren attach the same importance to the relationship and, should the grandparent–grandchild relationship be asymmetrical, what are the implications of this finding? It would not support the view that grandparents should be given a right of contact with their grandchildren when parents are opposed to this.

Further, this evidence shows that, in addition to the grandparent types identified by Neugarten and Weinstein (1964), Cherlin and Furstenberg (1985) or Mueller et al (2002), grandparents might also be classified according to the extent of their reluctance or enthusiasm for contact with their grandchildren (see Chapter Two of this book). Grandparenting is an extraordinarily diverse activity and the reluctant–enthusiastic grandparenting continuum appears to be a useful dimension for classifying grandparent behaviour.

FOUR

Activities with grandparents

Introduction

Our interviews sought to discover what happens when grandparents and grandchildren spend time together. Our focus in this chapter is on grandchildren who have regular face-to-face contact with grandparents and the importance they and their grandparents attach to the grandparent–grandchild relationship.

The grandparents' perceptions

Grandparents who saw their grandchildren regularly reported that they went shopping, shared meals, accompanied grandchildren on family outings, went for walks and talked to them about school and their other activities. There were few differences between maternal and paternal grandparents in the activities they shared with their grandchildren; however, seven in ten maternal grandparents (but no paternal grandparents) reported that they helped grandchildren with schoolwork. Two thirds of the maternal grandparents, but only one third of the paternal grandparents felt that they ever talked seriously to their grandchildren. It may be that helping grandchildren with learning or engaging them in serious conversation (particularly about family matters or other sensitive issues) was ill-suited to the role that some grandparents played. Paternal grandparents were less likely than maternal grandparents to enjoy the sustained contact that made these activities possible. They may also have wanted to avoid the accusation of interference in their grandchild's upbringing and preferred, therefore, to retain a light-hearted tone while their grandchildren were with them.

Half of the maternal grandparent group stated that they were involved in teaching or encouraging their grandchildren in hobbies, games and sports. Grandfathers reported that they were involved in outdoor sports, computing, country walks and active pursuits with their grandchildren, but grandmothers frequently restricted themselves to 'traditionally female' activities in the home. Although the paternal grandparents interviewed said that they did not help children with schoolwork, they were just as likely to report that they encouraged their grandchildren's leisure activities.

The focus of grandparents' attention

The evidence suggests that grandchildren, on their regular visits to their grandparents, were usually expected to amuse themselves by watching television or playing in the vicinity of their grandparents' home while their grandparents talked to their adult child. As a result, it was quite common for children to have reservations about their visits to their grandparents. When Wendy (aged 12) was asked, "Does grandma talk to you a lot when you go there?", she replied, "She's always busy. She never sits down".

Parents were aware of these feelings and recognised that grandchildren were not necessarily at the centre of their parents' attention. Tom's father, for example, observed that his mother was always busy and added, "She probably chats to me more when we go over but that's because they're teenagery types now". Annabel's grandfather, however, was among those who took a different point of view:

> Well, as far as the children are concerned, they have grown up and we have done all we can for them and they are all doing quite well and their children are fine and we look more towards the grandchildren than we do our own.

Among the 36 grandparents who were interviewed (21 maternal, 15 paternal), there were six who agreed that their children rather than their grandchildren were their priority, while seven suggested that their grandchildren were the priority. Most grandparents preferred not to make a choice but Wendy's maternal grandparents were not at all reticent. When asked whether their grandchildren occupied their thoughts as much as their own children, the maternal grandmother said, "Definitely not. The daughters mean more to me than the grandchildren".

Ann's relationship with her grandparents further illustrates the views of grandparents who see adult children rather than grandchildren as their main concern.

Ann's father commented that his mother was more comfortable with his three-year-old son and suggested that she was disappointed with Ann because she had learning difficulties. The paternal grandfather was described as 'more understanding' and did not share his wife's 'unrealistic expectations' for Ann's school progress and future career. He believed that both of his parents enjoyed being with the children but added: "they certainly show it in very different ways". When Ann's paternal grandmother was asked about the activities that she shared with her granddaughter, she seemed to confirm her son's view that she was a disappointed grandparent. On three occasions she made a reference to Ann's lack of concentration.

I've got a great big Snakes and Ladders which I put on the floor – a plastic one. But there again, with her, unfortunately, it's concentration and she does get frustrated about it.

Ann's mother had also noticed that her own parents preferred to spend time with her rather than with either of their grandchildren.

They don't have that much phone contact. My mum tends to phone to speak to me and I might pass her over to the children but I don't automatically think of it. When they [maternal grandparents] come here, they more often than not come here to see me rather than the children. I mean, the children are here, but my mum's happy to stand and talk to me in the kitchen rather than play with the children.

Affectionate relationships

Previous research has shown that grandparents generally want to be involved in the lives of their grandchildren (see, for example, Kornhaber, 1996; Dench et al, 1999). Grandchild–grandparent relationships are presented positively in the literature (Creasey, 1993; Schimoeller and Baranowski, 1998). In our study, grandparents often explained that their grandchildren were a source of joy and happiness; they were touched by their affection and amused by their activities and by the things they said. Grandparents are not only providers of love and protection but also have important symbolic functions. Bengtson (1985, p 24) suggests: "Grandparents are important simply because of their presence and what they mean for a family", and in our study, we discovered that some children felt strong ties of affection for grandparents which were not just related to fun-seeking and practical support.

A paternal grandfather, who had been seriously ill, was amused and delighted at his granddaughter's desire to look after him.

She will be sitting at the table with a colouring book or watching the television. She is 10 going on 65. She will suddenly get up, grab me by the hand and say, 'I think it is time you went for a walk'. There is a bench and she says, 'I think you must be tired so sit there', and then she will say, 'Have a smoke!'. I will roll a smoke and then she says, 'You have been here too long. Inside!'. And we go back in. (Jane's paternal grandfather)

In divorced families, grandparents may be especially important to young children because they represent stability in an otherwise disrupted family life.

I usually talk to my nanna. I have been having trouble at school. My report wasn't that good. I've got to do my writing because my writing's not very nice.... My nanna and Popsy, they are the best. (Eleanor, aged 9)

A mother described her younger daughter's affection for her grandfather in a way that was reminiscent of the Kivnick (1982) notion that children 'reinvolve' their grandparents with their past.

> She will sit on his lap. She will give him hugs and kisses. She will treat him like he's in his forties and not in his seventies. It's 'Give me piggy-backs' and 'Let's play horses'. (Marion's mother)

'Fun-seeking' grandparents

Chapter Two described the Neugarten and Weinstein (1964) classification of grandparent styles. One of their five grandparent types was called 'fun-seekers' – that is, grandparents who enjoy playful activities and see them as a central part of their activities with grandchildren. When Cherlin and Furstenberg (1985) classified grandparents, they concluded that fun-seekers did not emerge from their study because the grandchildren in their sample were aged 13-18 and Neugarten and Weinstein's (1964) sample contained younger children.

The fun-seeker grandparents in our study had grandchildren who were aged 8-16. Some grandparents (who were often but not always grandfathers) had a well-developed and fairly uninhibited sense of fun. Parents noted the presence or absence of this important quality in their own parents. One mother who reported that her parents were not particularly close to their grandchildren noted that her father was not a 'fun-seeker grandparent' and never had been. Her son, Peter (aged 15), was in regular contact with his grandparents on both sides of the family. He made the common adolescent complaint that visits to grandparents were boring, and remarked, "It is all right but I can't do it over long periods of time. It gets a bit boring".

When Peter's mother described her son's relationship with her father she commented,

> He's not a guy who goes for pleasure and fun but I think he's a responsible and a reliable grandfather. He was the same as a father.

Those grandparents who clearly fitted the 'fun-seeker' description (described by one 13-year-old boy as 'kiddy grandparents') were very popular with their grandchildren and described affectionately.

> We just play with him. We just play with his hair. He just leaves it all sticking up. (Debbie, aged 10)

Our only example of a grandmother who had been given care of her two grandchildren also claimed the fun-loving image that some grandparents seemed to cherish.

> They will say that I am mad.
>
> *Can you give me an example of that?*

I will dress up as a witch on Halloween. I'll do most things that they dare me to do. (Helen's maternal grandmother)

Elizabeth's grandmother lived 200 miles away from her granddaughter. She believed that their close relationship could be explained by the fact that she was more fun-loving than her granddaughter's older paternal grandmother who was in regular contact with her grandchild.

I think she just viewed me as a fun person.... My granddaughter viewed me especially as more fun than the other gran, because I do things, daft things with her, you know what I mean? I play with her, like I would with a playmate if you understand what I mean – you know, like a friend. (Elizabeth's maternal grandmother)

Len's mother had been married twice and had a new partner who lived with her and her two children for a few days each week. Len was her son from her first marriage. Len's stepfather no longer had contact with Len and had moved away to live with his parents. Len's maternal grandparents had always had a close relationship with Len and had helped him to cope with a variety of health problems and his distress during his mother's separation from his stepfather. These grandparents had earned a reputation for fun-seeking and their daughter explained that they had a talent for amusing their grandchildren.

They come down to the children's level. Everybody that knows my mum and my step-dad says the same thing – they're mad, you know. I think people admire the energy they have for a couple in their seventies, you know.... Yes, they are. They're barking!

Later in the interview she added:

Nanna's fun, she's not like everybody else. She's not.

What do you mean by that?

Because nanna does things. Like, nanna does funny things, when perhaps other nannas want to sit in the car and watch. (Len's mother)

When Len was interviewed, he first seemed to contradict, but then confirmed, his mother's view that his maternal grandparents were 'fun-seekers'. When he was asked what he did when he was with his grandparents, he said that he watched TV a lot.

Do you play any games or anything?

No. We go out for dinner. They are too old to play games.

What about quieter games, board games?

I play on my bampy's phone. There are games and things. I can find out things on his phone.

Later in the interview when he was explaining why he enjoyed his grandparents' company, he seemed then to confirm his mother's view of their 'fun' relationship.

You said that you enjoyed being with your nanna and bampy. So why do you like being with them?

Because they are quite fun people.

In what way?

They learn me loads of jokes and all that. (Len aged 12)

The grandparents were interviewed later the same day at their daughter's house when the grandfather had returned from work. As soon as they arrived, they made a number of light-hearted comments and seemed to have a 'double act' in which their daughter was the target of their good-natured humour. She commented, 'So you see what I have to put up with! I did warn you what they are like'.

These grandparents also talked about the serious side of their relationship and the help and advice they had given their grandson when it was discovered that Len had epilepsy. His maternal grandmother said:

Oh, he [Len] is very loving. Very loving, yes. He'd just put his arm around me and sometimes he says to me, 'Nan, I'm nearly as big as you and getting tall' and he'd give me a kiss and he says, 'You've got lovely smooth skin'.

This picture of loving and fun-loving grandparents was not an uncommon one. Close and loving relationships brought happiness both to grandchildren and to grandparents who were able to enjoy frequent contact with their grandchildren. There were also examples of fun-seeking grandparents with teenage grandchildren. They seemed to have adapted their fun-seeking to fit their older grandchildren's interests.

Positive relationships with older grandchildren

Some older grandparents and their grandchildren had close and loving relationships.

Belinda (aged 15) visited her only grandparent – her paternal grandmother – every day because her grandmother lived near her school. She explained that she discussed her problems with her grandmother, slept at her house regularly and enjoyed her company. Her mother, who was not interviewed, had left the family home and her father had become the resident parent. Belinda spent much of her time looking after her grandmother but, despite this, she explained that she felt that she was like a mother to her.

We have more of a mother/daughter relationship than a grandparent really 'cos we're closer than anybody else. (Belinda)

Linda (aged 10) called to see her widowed maternal grandmother several times each week and slept at her house at the weekends. Linda's grandmother was disabled and was not responsible for looking after her grandchild. When Linda described her relationship with her maternal grandmother, she said:

We had a good laugh the other night when *Who Wants to be a Millionaire?* was on. I was trying to have a guess, because my nan was always getting in before me and I thought, 'Give me a go!' and we kept on laughing. We play cards and we do loads of things together. Quizzes, I have got a keyboard down there, because she used to play and things like that.... Yes and she helps me if I do things wrong [on the keyboard] and things like that.

What do you talk about?

Just everything, everything really.

Diana (aged 14) felt protective towards her widowed maternal grandmother who was in her seventies and lived on her own. She also visited her grandmother on her way home from school and saw her at the weekends. Diana explained that she cared deeply about her grandmother.

When I leave my nan on her own, I think, 'Has she locked the door?' and things like that. But you don't worry about your mum not remembering to do that. I think my grandmother thinks about us. I think she cares and she sends us presents and things like that and phones us.... When she phones and says things like 'I'm thinking of you' I think, 'Ah that's really nice and she is lovely'. When we go down there to the house there are hundreds of photos of us so yeah I do think she cares.

The negative correlations that have been established in previous research between grandparent or grandchild age and the quality of grandchildren's relationships may have masked determinants of grandchild–grandparent relationships that depended on the coincidence of a number of circumstances. In these three cases, the favourable conditions were grandparents' gender (grandmother), widowhood, mother's and sibling's absence when the visits took place, grandchild's gender (granddaughter), frequent opportunities for visits and no major childcare responsibilities for grandmother. Parents, divorced mothers particularly, may unwittingly become a barrier to close grandparent–grandchild relationships. It might be mothers' need for attention or older women's desire to give priority to their daughters that provides the explanation. Parental divorce may not be an important influence because these close relationships had been formed before the children's parents had divorced although it is possible that family strife, that predated parental separation, was a factor in bringing these granddaughters closer to their grandmothers. Loneliness would provide a reason for these grandmothers to form a special relationship with their favourite granddaughter. It was 'an exchange' that added to the security and happiness of both grandmother and grandchild. The reasons why so many grandparents appeared to be 'adult' rather than 'child-centred' and the nature of the special relationships discussed here between older grandmothers and their granddaughters merit further investigation.

Grandchildren's reservations about their grandparents

Grandchildren who were in regular contact with their grandparents described an affectionate relationship but some older grandchildren in particular had reservations and made sharply critical comments. For example, 11-year-old Valerie had little sympathy for her maternal grandmother who was in poor health.

> She's a bit of a hypochondriac. Like sometimes, maybe she's ill – because she gets a bit ill – and she has to have tablets but she takes it a bit too far.

Steve (aged 14) made a complaint that was common among adolescent grandchildren when he explained that visits to his grandparents' house were "boring". Grandchildren explained that, on occasions, they had to be persuaded to visit their grandparents because there was 'nothing to do' at their grandparents' house. Len's comments about his paternal step-grandmother were particularly harsh:

> She's the kind of woman who would just sit in the chair and watch TV all day. She would rather clean the house [than spend time with me]. (Len, aged 12)

Other grandchildren may have been kinder, but the perception was often the same: grandparents do not give enough attention to their grandchildren.

Grandparents who were overburdened with family responsibilities (see Chapter Ten) often agreed that grandparenting should be about pleasurable experiences and not about childcare and discipline. They believed that grandparents, irrespective of gender or lineage, should be free to enjoy their relationship with their grandchildren. Grandchildren's comments, however, tended to support the view that mothering rather than 'grandmothering' was

Activities with grandparents

the priority for many older women and nine- and ten-year-old grandchildren and adolescents aged 13 or 14 gave similar accounts. They liked to see their grandparents and said that they felt affection for them; but they also felt ignored and were sometimes bored in their company.

Robert, aged 14, rarely saw his father, had no paternal grandparents and visited his widowed maternal grandmother once each month when he and his mother spent the whole day at her home. Their regular journeys by car took about an hour. Robert was asked what he did when he visited his grandmother.

> Eat, watch TV, play on the computer. Sometimes I go out to the park and stuff like that. Sometimes I go with my mum. Sometimes I go with my friend. Sometimes I go on my own. When she came down here a couple of times we used to go out to [name of town]. But when I'm up there, she doesn't take me out anywhere now, 'cos she does a lot of housework and like cooking for us – or whatever – when we're down there.

Debbie (aged 10) saw her maternal grandparents three or four times each week but was unable to think of specific activities that she shared with her grandparents on these occasions. She commented, "My mum just sits and chats to my nan".

> Edward was 10 years old and he and his younger brother were in regular contact with their maternal grandmother and their paternal grandparents who lived nearby. When Edward was asked what he did when he visited his grandmother's house, he replied that he watched television and played with his brother. Edward did not express much enthusiasm for visiting his grandparents but preferred the company of his maternal grandmother.
>
> *Do you like to spend time with this [maternal] grandmother?*
>
> Yes.
>
> *Can you say why?*
>
> It makes my mum happy and we just don't get so bored then.
>
> *What about going to see your other [paternal] grandparents? Is it nice?*
>
> A bit boring.
>
> *Why is that?*
>
> There's nothing to do there and they haven't got any fun things to do.

> *What would be a fun thing to do then?*
>
> Sometimes it's fun because if it's a special occasion, my cousins are over there too.
>
> *What if your cousins are not there?*
>
> I just watch TV and play with my brother.
>
> When Edward was pressed for more information about the activities he enjoyed with his maternal grandmother, he said that he enjoyed playing board games but had only done this "once or twice when we got really fed up and bored".
>
> This child's maternal grandmother was asked whether she took part in any activities with her grandchildren and replied,
>
> Not so much now, because when I look after them they are doing their own thing more or less.

Wendy (aged 12) reported that she got on well with her maternal grandparents and enjoyed visiting them. When her mother was interviewed, however, she wanted to talk about Wendy's brother (aged 15) who did not have a close relationship with his maternal grandparents. This mother's comments provided a useful reminder to those who might want to conclude that 'adult-oriented' grandparents are letting their grandchildren down. She observed that the grandparent–grandchild relationship is a two-way process and depends on grandchildren as well as grandparents playing their part.

> I think my dad has tried. Yes he has. He's tried to do things. They [her father and her 15-year-old son] went to a football match once because my dad is into football. But my son is not at all sporty and I think he fell asleep through the football match. He [grandfather] likes to take him up the garden to his shed to show him things that he's been working on but I don't think that he is really interested. What can you do?

When the maternal grandfather was interviewed, he explained that he wanted to share some of his skills and experience with his grandson but had been unable to capture his interest

> I'd love to try to get him [his 15-year-old grandson] involved in doing something practically but unfortunately nowadays computers have taken over and kids only want to watch television or play with computers. They don't want to make anything by hand.

It could be argued that the best grandparents are those who are skilled at finding ways of amusing and interesting their grandchildren. When (as in the case of Wendy's brother) there is a mismatch between a grandparent's and a grandchild's interests, the onus is on the grandparent to find out more about the grandchild and the activities that he or she might enjoy. Robert's grandmother provided a very different perspective on the question and Charles' relationship with his maternal grandfather also threw new light on the phenomenon of 'adult-oriented' grandparents and the 'generation gap' that appears to affect grandparent–grandchild relationships.

Robert (who observed that his maternal grandmother got on with cooking and housework) lived 30 miles away from his grandmother's home. Robert's mother, although she was not asked about this directly, took the opportunity in the interview to explain why her mother did not engage in much activity with her son.

I think, if they were together longer she would [pay more attention to him]. She likes to play games. I know she does with her other grandson. But we're just not there long enough for her to do that.

Robert's grandmother who was about to celebrate her 80th birthday explained that her 14-year-old grandson liked to "do his own thing" and that on his regular visits with his mother he was bored. She added, "He's just that age".

He's growing up now and he's building his own life now. He's got his friends where he sleeps over and they sleep over with him. When it's his birthday, they go to these places where they have pizzas and things.... He's bloodthirsty and likes all these awful films. We're gradually getting a few here. He chooses and I have to buy it. He got this one that had '18' on which I didn't notice and the lady said, 'I'm afraid he can't buy it', so I had to accept it and put it in my bag.

When Robert was interviewed, he said that he was close to his grandmother. He then added, "Well, it's not exactly close, because we don't see each other, like every week or something like that, but we do see each other once every month, so we're kind of close".

Robert's grandmother indicated that she and her grandchild inhabited two very different worlds and this generation gap can be a difficult one to bridge. What can an elderly, widowed grandmother do to prevent her teenage grandson from being bored? Grandparenting changes as grandchildren and grandparents age and older grandparents may not have the energy or the resources to keep teenage grandchildren amused.

Few children said that they did not like their grandparents but expressions of affection were often accompanied by critical comments. The relationship between Charles (aged

13) and his maternal grandparents provided a good illustration. Charles preferred to spend time with his paternal grandparents because they, unlike his maternal grandparents, seemed enthusiastic about sharing his company. His maternal and paternal grandparents lived near to each other but they were both an hour's drive from their grandchild's home. The paternal grandfather reported that he enjoyed fishing, clay pigeon shooting and football with his grandson but the maternal grandparents' interview suggested that they were not engaged in much activity either with their grandson in the divorced family or with their other younger grandchildren. Charles spoke affectionately about his father's parents and said he felt "a really close bond". Charles' mother suggested that he would be "on cloud nine" when he knew he was going to see his paternal grandparents.

I go over there and stay there for three or four days. Sometimes, I go over there at the weekends and they take me out fishing and that. (Charles)

What's that relationship [with your maternal grandparents] like?

It's sort of not very strong because they love their garden so much. If I go there, I'm not allowed to do anything. I'm not even allowed to go outside because they are doing something to their garden. We go out somewhere boring, or they go out to a garden place and buy plants.

You actually feel a bit bored when you are there?

Yes. There's nothing wrong with them. They're fine. I have to make myself do something if I'm on my own. It's not really fun when you're on your own is it? I've got to, like muck around in the back garden doing something. But I'm not allowed to touch any of the plants. No, not the Azaleas or whatever they are called. Can't touch them.

His mother said:

My parents are a bit besotted with their garden because they are always out there in the garden and my dad is out there putting in the shrubs and runner beans and pottering around there. My mum is more with her feet on the ground and, although she is totally devoted to her grandson, she is more down to earth. To be fair to her, the other grandparents are older, retired earlier and have more time to devote to him and only up until recently they only had one grandchild to be besotted by. Whereas my mother has five grandchildren so she has had more to contend with. So you can't really compare them. He really loves them the same but different.

Charles expressed affection for both his maternal and paternal grandparents and recognised that his relationships with his grandparents had changed as he and they got older. He had no contact with his father and his paternal grandparents were among those that might easily have lost contact with their grandson if they had not been able to maintain a close relationship with their ex-daughter-in-law (see Chapter Ten). He clearly preferred the company of his 'fun-seeking' paternal grandparents but his mother could not quite admit it. The maternal grandparents were also not willing to admit that they did not engage in much activity with Charles or with their other grandchildren. Their contact with their grandson and the activities that they shared had been affected by distance, their own interests and their grandchild's age but in this, and in other cases, there was little evidence that divorce had changed grandparents' approaches to grandparenting.

The parents in our study had been divorced for two or four years. It is possible that 'adult-oriented' grandparents still felt anxious about their divorced children and wanted to talk to them more frequently. Without a comparison group of grandparents in intact families, however, it is not possible to assess this. Older children were more likely to complain about their visits to grandparents but nine- and ten-year-olds also expressed reservations. This research project did not include interviews with children under the age of eight and it is recognised that grandparents probably behave differently with younger grandchildren.

The adult-centred/child-centred continuum

We have identified a further continuum that might be part of a system for classifying grandparents: the adult-centred/child-centred continuum (Table 2). At one pole of the continuum were grandparents who organised events and activities and spent their time in the company of their grandchildren. At the other extreme were those who expected grandchildren to amuse themselves while they spent time talking to their divorced son or daughter. The continuum has a midpoint of 'family-centred grandparents' who concentrated their attention neither on adults nor children but on catering for the family group.

Among the child-centred grandparents, grandfathers excelled at horseplay and games with younger children and organised events that were planned specifically for their grandchildren. There were examples of grandmothers who shared children's interests in playing musical instruments or painting, for

Table 2: The adult-centred/child-centred continuum in grandparenting

Adult-centred	Family-centred	Child-centred
Focus on parent	Attention to family group	Focus on child
Adult conversation	Catering meals, snacks	Play, fun, games
Grandchild ignored	Little individual attention	Child centre of attention
Grandchild bored	Grandchild bored	Grandchild stimulated
Affectionate relationships with grandchildren	Affectionate relationships with grandchildren	Affectionate relationships with grandchildren

example, and shopping trips when clothes or toys would be bought for the grandchild.

Concluding comment

Grandchildren's descriptions of spending time with their grandparents were often accompanied by accounts of the presents, outings and activities that were an important part of the experience of sharing their grandparents' company. Some children in this study felt that they were largely ignored when they made their regular visits to their grandparents' homes. Others enjoyed affectionate relationships that enriched their own lives and those of their grandparents. Neugarten and Weinstein (1964), Cherlin and Furstenberg (1985), Mueller et al (2002) and others have noted that grandparenting is a diverse activity. Our study suggests that it is important in accounting for this diversity to discover whether grandparents' main priorities are their adult children or their grandchildren – in other words, where they might be positioned on the adult-centred/child-centred continuum. Grandparents' personal styles and their skills in relating to children are also determinants of the quality of their relationships with grandchildren and 'fun-seekers' were invariably the most popular grandparents. However, there was also an interesting finding about special relationships (see Linda, Belinda and Diana) between granddaughters and their older widowed grandmothers.

FIVE

Discipline and favouritism

This chapter considers the issues of child discipline and favouritism and 'the rules' that apply to the relationship between grandparents and their grandchildren. It asks:

- Does the 'norm of non-interference' mean that grandparents should hesitate to discipline their grandchildren?
- Do grandparents often 'spoil' grandchildren, and do parents object to the grandparents' indulgence and lax discipline?
- Are there rules about reprimanding grandchildren when a parent is present?
- Are grandparents who have been asked to provide regular childcare given free rein to discipline their grandchildren as if they were their own children?
- Do parents feel resentful when they learn that their ex-spouse's parents have reprimanded their child for bad behaviour?

Disciplining grandchildren

Parents, grandchildren and grandparents were asked to describe their experience and discuss their feelings about discipline and childcare. We anticipated that discipline might be a contentious subject but found that it was a source of conflict in few of the families that were interviewed. Some grandparents felt unsure about whether they should rebuke their grandchildren for bad behaviour, but few parents saw this as an issue. Only two of the 35 resident parents who were interviewed expressed strong reservations about their own parents' disciplinary practices. For example, Eleanor's mother, whose views are also discussed in Chapter Ten of this book, commented:

> The other thing, there, is that my dad takes it upon himself to discipline them when I'm there. That's something I don't like. Not when I'm there. I feel that I should be left to deal with it when I'm there. If I'm not, then fine.

There were, however, other resident parents who had reservations about grandparents' *lack* of discipline. Janet's mother noted that her nine-year-old daughter and her younger brother were in the habit of seeking their grandparents' permission for things that their mother had already refused to grant.

> They just ask her [maternal grandmother] for anything and she'll cave in, even if I said no. They're not allowed to have it but she'll just cave in.

Ingrid's mother also noted that her parents did not discipline her three children as much as she felt they should:

> I have on occasions explained to my parents that it's no good just me disciplining the children. If they want them to be well behaved with them, then they have to accept responsibility for their discipline.

Tony's mother believed that the maternal grandmother had a duty to adopt childcare practices that were compatible with her own views about bringing up children. She used an example of 'telling tales' to illustrate the point.

> She always had this thing when we were growing up about telling tales. She would say, 'Don't tell tales! Go away'. I said to her, 'Don't say that to mine because I don't like that expression. Children should always be able to tell the person who is looking after them. If they can't come to you who can they tell?'.

Among the 14 non-resident parents (all fathers), two had some reservations about maternal grandparents' discipline – or lack of it – and one was concerned about the disciplinary practices of his own parents.

> I used to say to her – she had a bad habit – me sticking somebody in their place [that is, disciplining one of the children], telling them off or something, and then she would console them, like. I would say, 'There ain't no good me telling them off if you're going to them and saying, 'Come and have a sweet'. (Zoe's father discussing his disagreements with his mother)

Paternal grandparents

Fifteen of the 35 resident parents either said that their ex-spouse had no parents or that they were unable to comment on the grandparents' relationship with their children. Another 15 reported that they were happy for their ex- spouse's parents to reprimand their children when they misbehaved. Surprisingly, no mother raised any serious objection to the disciplinary practices of the *paternal* grandparents, although they were described on occasions as 'soft' and by one mother as 'Spockish' (in a reference to the liberal thinking of the 1960s; see Spock, 1958). Five mothers claimed that the question had never arisen, as far as they were aware, because the paternal grandparents would not have needed to tell their well-behaved children about bad behaviour. George's mother believed the explanation was that the paternal grandparents' relationship with the children was rather formal and, in this atmosphere, they were disinclined to misbehave.

> The children are always on their best behaviour when they go over there [to their paternal grandparents' house]. It's just for a visit. If they were at my

parents' house, they might feel relaxed and at home very much more and they might sit with their feet up on the furniture. But I don't think they'd do that at [ex-husband's] parents' house so they wouldn't ever need to be disciplined. They'd be behaving themselves and listening and having their cup of tea. It's a different sort of atmosphere from my mum and dad's house where they can let themselves go.

Both mothers and fathers suggested that paternal grandparents were less likely to reprimand their children and were more likely to believe that the right approach was to draw a parent's attention to misbehaviour and avoid getting involved. For example, paternal grandparents whose grandchildren 'showed off' in front of their friends and were rude to them were not reprimanded. These grandparents decided to say nothing at the time and report the matter to their son. Our evidence suggested that maternal grandparents would be more inclined to reprimand the grandchildren. The probable explanation is that paternal grandparents see their grandchildren intermittently but maternal grandparents more frequently see themselves as part of the family group, that is, sharing the responsibility for children's upbringing.

Mothers were usually unconcerned or even pleased that their parents and ex-parents-in-law were willing to help with discipline. They rarely appeared to be in conflict with grandparents but remembered occasions when grandparents had overreacted or grumbled about children's behaviour unnecessarily. Fathers were just as ready to accept that grandparents should intervene when children were behaving badly. However, they also confirmed that paternal grandparents usually do much less to discipline their grandchildren than maternal grandparents.

My parents wouldn't [tell the children off] so much. I think K's [ex-wife's] mother would have been more mindful to be snappy with them, to put them in order. I think she's a bit over the top, she's a bit fiery and then it settles down. When she's fiery, she says things that she doesn't mean. But she's fine with the kids. (Tom's father)

They try and give more love than discipline. They leave that to me and they kind of say, 'You sort it out'. (Oliver's father)

Pat's father was asked if his parents would reprimand his daughter.

No, they wouldn't do it. They think that's my role or my ex-wife's. As regards to her [ex-wife's] mother, I don't know. I have heard her telling her off [Pat, aged 11], putting her in her place.

Was that okay with you?

Yes. I think she's got her head screwed on and if the girl deserved it, she deserved it.

A resident father expressed similar views but pointed out that his mother had had to assume a great deal of responsibility for childcare and, as a result, his children treated their paternal grandmother like a parent.

> I do think that she's got the right [to discipline her grandchildren] but I think the relationship has changed in the sense that they treat her more like a mother now. So they argue with her, and Belinda, particularly, went through a stage where she argued about everything. If you said that the sky was blue, she'd have argued that it was green. So because they looked on her like a mother, they argued like a teenager would argue. (Belinda's father)

Children simply accepted grandparental discipline as a fact of life. Their comments seemed to confirm that adults of both generations showed a united front against rudeness, destructiveness, fighting with siblings and all forms of minor misbehaviour.

> *Suppose you were at your grandparent's house and your mum was with you. Would your grandparents still tell you off?*
>
> Yes, but my parents would shout as well. (Kate, aged 9)

A child who had no contact with her paternal grandparents noted that her maternal grandparents' discipline needed to improve. She felt that her own behaviour was, of course, beyond reproach but suggested that her grandparents were not firm enough with her brother and sister who were aged eight and nine.

> J and A get a bit naughty sometimes and they get away with it, so I think something should be done really. (Clare, aged 14)

Her mother, like other mothers in this study, had no concerns about grandparent discipline but thought that her mother was 'quite strict' at times.

> Absolutely no problem. I mean, if they deserved it, then yes. And she wouldn't tell them off for nothing, you know. (Clare's mother)

Trust and conflict

Some grandparents (especially paternal grandparents) were worried about reprimanding their grandchildren for their misdemeanours. Most parents, however, trusted grandparents to discipline their children appropriately. While parents recognised that there were times when their children deserved to be reprimanded, they were implacably opposed to grandparents smacking them even if they themselves did so on occasions. They added that their children's grandparents would not dream of hitting their children but still wanted to make the point during the interview. A grandfather or grandmother who did smack a grandchild could expect to trigger a family conflict, especially if the mother's relationship with the grandparent was not a close one. Again it was Eleanor's mother who had the strongest views.

> She [maternal grandmother] knows not to hit my children because I'd kill her. Well, I'd make sure that she wouldn't do it again. It's not that I don't believe in spanking....

We wanted to find out whether or not grandparent favouritism should be handled with the same equanimity as discipline. Would parents' understanding and restraint desert them when they felt that their parents or their ex-parents-in-law had a favourite grandchild?

Favourite grandchildren

Favouritism was common in our study with many grandparents admitting that they had a favourite grandchild. Of the 36 interviews with grandparents, no fewer than 22 (13 maternal and 9 paternal grandparents) provided evidence of a favourite grandchild. Six maternal and five paternal grandparents reported that they had no favourites. Other grandparents had only one grandchild or gave an answer that could not be classified. Favoured grandchildren were not always the children in the divorced families studied here and one set of grandparents told us that their favourite grandchild lived in Australia.

Despite the surprising honesty of most grandparents, there were some who were embarrassed by the question.

> Charles' paternal grandparents denied that they had favourites, but their statements seemed to point to some ambivalence and an uncertainty about how such a question should be answered. These grandparents had three grandchildren. Their grandson was 13 years old. Their son had remarried and now had two young children with whom they had infrequent contact. Their reply seemed to be anticipating a time when their grandson would be growing up and growing away from them and they would, they hoped, be closer to their new grandchildren. They seemed to be hedging their bets and planning to re-deploy their grandparenting energies to secure their future grandparenting role when their grandson might have outgrown them.
>
> Charles, however, had few doubts about the fact that he was their favourite grandchild and explained:
>
> > I guess it's because I'm number-one son. I was the first of the pack. I was the first in the family and we didn't have anybody that could override me. I'm the oldest.

Although two grandmothers and one grandfather admitted to favourites, their respective spouses disagreed (this question was put to each of them separately when the other was not present). There were occasional signs of reluctance to answer the question, which was seen as a sensitive one.

> *Is there one that is special to you for any reason?*
>
> That's a loaded question but no, I think it is them and us. And I know that if there was a problem they all can come to us for help. (Steve's maternal step-grandfather)

Despite feeling uncomfortable in admitting that she had a favourite grandchild, Janet's maternal grandmother decided to answer the question.

> *Is there one of the three of them that's special to you for any reason?*
>
> I shouldn't answer that should I? Yes, it's Janet.

While grandparents were sometimes prepared – if a little hesitant on occasions – to admit that they had favourite grandchildren, they were careful to qualify their favouritism by adding that they treated all their grandchildren equally. And when a mother suspected that her parents were more attached to one of her children than the other, this was tolerated provided that the grandparents hid their feelings. It was what grandparents did and did not do rather than what they thought or felt that mattered to parents.

> Mum and dad have made a point that they treat all the grandchildren the same, even though my three are in their immediate world. They have another three in [Town A] and another one in [Town B]. They're all treated the same as regards birthday presents and Christmas presents. They all have the same amount spent on them. (Alfie's mother. In their interview, these grandparents said that they did not have favourites)
>
> Oh definitely, my mother has got four grandchildren. My brother has got two children. And like I said, when they are together they are all treated the same. If one has ten pence, the four of them have ten pence. And that is something I have always said and my brother has always said. But, I shouldn't say it, but yes my mother, and she would admit it, has a favourite: Linda. (Linda's mother)

First-born grandchildren often had a special place in grandparents' affections but younger children could also be favourites. When circumstances meant that a particular grandchild had had an unusually large amount of contact with his or her grandparents, this was also likely to become a 'special' relationship. A grandmother explained why one of her granddaughters in an intact family was her favourite grandchild. She also recalled her feelings about grandparent favouritism when she was the mother of young children.

> She is [the favourite], because she was my first grandchild. I don't believe in favourites and I used to get very cross with my mother because my son was her absolute favourite. But I have to confess that she [her daughter's child in an intact family] is the most vulnerable and therefore my heart is very close to her. (Ingrid's paternal grandmother)

Some grandparents did not feel guilty about having a favourite and simply explained why one of their grandchildren had become closer to them than others.

> But she [a grandchild in another family] is lovely and she is special. I was in the hospital the day she was born and I saw her have her first wash about an hour after she was born and that was great. It was as if she was mine. I never had that with my own. (Jane's paternal grandmother)

Alan's grandmother had a favourite grandchild who was not one of the children in the divorced family.

> Well he [Alan's cousin] is [a favourite grandchild] of course. We thought we had lost him when he was in intensive care for more than a week. He was just two days old when he got ill. (Alan's maternal grandmother)

Alan's mother, however, did not seem to be aware of this and named Alan's sister as her parents' favourite grandchild.

> I suppose K, the eldest one, had the most special relationship because she had nanny and granddad to herself for a time.... So she's got especially fond memories of all that. But I don't think they did really, I think they tried to treat them as equals.

Parents' responses

Valerie's mother believed that her mother had a favourite. She did not seem particularly concerned, as her mother had been careful to hide this from her children.

> I think it's N. Maybe it's just because he's a boy, or there's something about him that she likes. But she doesn't show it really. We just know.

Linda's mother suggested that Linda was her maternal grandmother's favourite grandchild but was, nevertheless, upset that her ex-husband's parents also had a favourite grandchild. She explained:

> One of my rules is that they've got a package deal.

Two mothers were angry because they believed that their children were being treated unequally.

> I had problems when I had M [her first child]. His mother [the paternal grandmother] had only had three boys. So when I had M, I could understand that she sort of doted on M and that she was the apple of her eye. But when I had E [her son] she would not even hold him. She would walk out of the room with M and leave E in the middle of the floor crying his eyes out. She used to send M birthday and Christmas cards and presents but not the others and now she has stopped doing that. (Karen's mother)

Karen's father viewed his mother's favouritism differently but his version of events seemed to be another interpretation of the same facts.

> She took to my daughter, but when the boy arrived, I mean, it was a bit too much for her to have the two and my wife couldn't compromise there. She thought that my mother was, you know, pushing him [her grandson] to one side. But she wasn't. She was used to having the girl from an early age. But two would have been too much and my wife caused difficulties there. Well before the end [of the marriage] there was a rift between her [wife] and my mother.

He added:

> I had just come in from work and they [his mother and his wife] were eager to have a go at each other. [My ex-wife] was attacking my mother verbally and, you know, my mother had taken umbrage then because, you know.

> *And then did that stop your mother seeing the children?*

> She did effectively, yes. Except on the rare occasions that I used to take the children up to see her, which became more infrequent. (Karen's father)

Helen's family was unusual because the court granted a residence order to the maternal grandmother who was now wholly responsible for her grandchildren. Helen's father reported:

> Well my wife didn't even like her own daughter. She adored D [son] but didn't get on with Helen her daughter. I don't know why. So she [Helen, aged 10] used to stay with her nan.

Helen's mother claimed that since the maternal grandmother had been granted a residence order, Helen's younger brother had replaced Helen as her maternal grandmother's favourite grandchild. The grandmother's explanation for her apparent favouritism was:

I never saw D [Helen's brother] very much at all really when he was younger because he was very much a mummy's boy and he wanted to stay with mummy all the time.

Concluding comments

There is a temptation in an exploratory study of this kind to want to identify issues that people feel strongly about. A 'non-issue' that generates few strong feelings and produces a variety of moderate statements might be seen as less fertile ground. However, should we be surprised that grandparent discipline and favouritism were not generally a source of conflict in the families studied here?

Teachers, playground assistants, youth club leaders and even the driver of the school bus may reprimand children on occasions. Parents do not often object to those in authority issuing mild rebukes to their children when they are misbehaving. Grandparents on both sides of the family share some responsibility for children on occasions and parents accept that they have the right to reprimand their children. Perhaps we should not have been surprised that grandparent discipline was not often a contentious issue for children or their divorced parents in our sample or that parents and ex-parents-in-law did not allow their partisan feelings to influence their judgements. Mothers often enrolled their own parents as child carers and expected them to play a role in child socialisation. Their ex-husband's parents usually felt that they had to 'tread carefully', but mothers often knew little about the events that took place when their children visited their ex-spouse's parents. Children did not talk about their visits (see Chapter Eight) and resident parents did not ask questions.

However, parents were often irritated when they felt that a grandparent had 'undermined' them by sympathising with a child that had been reprimanded for bad behaviour. None of the parents wanted grandparents to smack their children even if, on occasions, they did so themselves. Resident parents often wanted their parents to share the responsibility for disciplining their children and did not object to their ex-husband's parents reprimanding their grandchildren when they were in their care.

Parents were more circumspect and somewhat ambivalent about grandparents' favouritism. Many grandparents had a favourite grandchild, who might or might not be in the divorced family, and acknowledged this in the interviews. Parents sometimes suspected that this was so but did not want grandparents to discuss it with them and certainly did not want their children to be made aware of it. Grandparents, they concluded, must treat children equally. In fact, grandparents on both sides of divorced families were careful to do this and most said that they ensured that their grandchildren received presents of equal value and, when the children were with them, that they gave them roughly the same amount of attention.

The study demonstrated a considerable degree of consensus in most parents' and grandparents' views about bringing up children, but this might be explained by the fact that grandparents felt obliged to observe parents' wishes. Dench and Ogg's (2002) analysis of the 1998 British Social Attitudes Survey data includes discussion of the influence that grandparents felt they had on the upbringing of grandchildren and the extent of their agreement about bringing up children. The authors noted that higher levels of agreement were not necessarily symptomatic of close relationships but simply reflected grandparents' inability to influence decisions about their grandchildren's upbringing:

> Both groups of respondents (parents and grandparents) may have been influenced by the idea that grandparents should not really have much say, and that where they do – or certainly where it is publicised – this risks breaking the golden rule of non-interference. (Dench and Ogg, 2002, p 100)

It was not surprising, therefore, that this study found that, with some notable exceptions, grandparent discipline and favouritism were areas of agreement rather than sources of conflict. Grandparents did not report that they had entered into an explicit negotiation with parents about how they should behave, but had considered the problems nevertheless. It may be that they wanted to comply with parents' wishes to avoid conflict and some may have adopted practices that fitted in with what they perceived to be the resident parent's opinions. This interpretation is compatible with the view that grandparenting is a mediated relationship (see Chapter Two of this book).

SIX

The main grandparents

Introduction

Once parents separate, grandparents on the mother's side of the family often play a more significant role in supporting their daughter and caring for grandchildren (Dench and Ogg, 2002, p 55), and maternal grandmothers often have a more influential role than their husbands, the maternal grandfathers. Other research (Aldous, 1985; Mills et al, 2001; Roberto et al, 2001) has concluded that both maternal and paternal grandmothers' relationships with their grandchildren are different in quality from those of their husbands who are often less involved in childcare. Some grandparents in our study claimed that they conducted their grandparenting as 'a couple' or a 'grandparenting unit'. Although they saw their grandchildren on the same occasions, however, the *quality* of that contact might be a different matter (see Cherlin and Furstenberg, 1992, p 118).

These factors have led to a conception of a 'grandparenting hierarchy' in which grandmothers are ranked more highly than grandfathers and maternal grandparents take priority over paternal grandparents (see Chapter Two of this book). Although this hierarchy is well established in the literature (Eisenberg, 1988; Creasey and Koblewski, 1991; Uhlenberg and Hammill, 1998; Findler, 2000), it is still important to ask, 'Why does it exist?'. Is it simply that maternal grandparents, particularly in divorced families, have more opportunities to forge closer relationships?

Maternal and paternal grandparenting

Chan and Elder (2000) concluded that close relationships between grandchildren and their maternal grandparents could be explained by mothers' relationships with their parents. It is a view that is echoed in our study by George's father, who believed that this explained the differences that existed in the quality of the maternal and paternal grandparents' relationships in his family.

George (aged 14) lived with his mother and his older sister. The children saw their father on Sundays and on most weekdays when he picked them up by car from school. George's father visited his parents for a short time every Sunday to collect Sunday lunch, which he reheated when he returned home. However, the children rarely accompanied him on these brief visits. Although the grandparents on both sides of the family lived close to their grandchildren's home, the paternal grandparents had much less contact than George's maternal grandparents.

George's father explained that his children did not always want to accompany him on his visits to collect the food. He felt that this was normal for adolescent grandchildren and further explained the difference in contact as an inevitable consequence of his wife's close relationship with her mother.

I suppose they were always close because it was like my wife's mum and they [his wife and children] would obviously go round there a lot more, especially when she was at home after having the children. So I suppose they are always going to be closer.

This suggests that paternal grandparents do not volunteer for second place but are usually overshadowed by maternal grandparents who have gained an advantage as a result of their close ties with their daughter (see Mueller et al, 2002, p 381). Maternal grandmothers, in particular, often have more frequent contact with mothers because they may visit their daughter and young grandchildren during the day at times when fathers and grandfathers may be at work. It is not surprising, therefore, that grandchildren often grow up with closer relationships with their maternal grandparents and particularly with maternal grandmothers. This indicates that 'matrilineal advantage' (see Mills et al, 2001, p 430) may be simply a question of taking opportunities that are not usually available to paternal grandparents.

Peter (aged 15) was aware of this restriction on his paternal grandparents' opportunities for contact and he commented on how it affected his relationship with them. Absence, he concluded, makes the heart grow less fond.

Was the relationship with your mum's parents different in any way before your parents' split up?

It was less close than now. I live with my mum, so more often I'm going to see my mum's parents rather than my other grandparents.

Did it make any difference to your dad's parents?

Yeah, I don't see them [paternal grandparents] as much. I'm not as close as I was with them. I don't see my dad as much.

Comparing parents' and grandchildren's accounts

Mothers were asked to comment specifically on whether they believed the maternal and paternal grandparents were 'very close', 'close', 'not close' or 'not at all close' to the target grandchild in the divorced family. More than eight in ten mothers (28 of the 33 mothers) reported that their children were 'close' or 'very close' to their maternal grandmothers. However, only about four in ten grandchildren (11 out of 27) were said to be 'close' or 'very close' to their paternal grandmothers. These mothers did not make a distinction between maternal grandmothers and grandfathers, but reported that only three in ten paternal grandfathers were close to their grandchildren.

Sixteen of the 30 grandchildren, who were interviewed, said that they had a good relationship with, or wanted to be closer to their paternal grandparents. Only four grandchildren volunteered the fact that they did not like their paternal grandparents. Among the other 10 grandchildren, some either did not have paternal grandparents, did not know their paternal grandparents or did not comment.

Marion's mother (who described her children's relationship with their maternal grandparents as "absolutely brilliant") went on to describe their relationship with a paternal grandmother who had recently died.

> It was very good. We saw her [paternal grandmother] most days for an hour or so. It wasn't the same sort of relationship that my parents had. But then I sometimes think it's often slightly different with the husband's family than with the daughter's. She would cuddle them, buy them sweets. She was very interested in what they did. His father liked to see the children, but there wasn't that bond there. He wasn't the sort of person that got very close or was very demonstrative of his affections or anything like that.

This mother portrayed the relationship with the paternal grandparents as less important than that with the maternal grandparents, even though her description of grandparent–grandchild relationships did not indicate this. The perception that it was often 'slightly different' with grandparents on the father's side of the family was shared by other mothers in the group.

Barbara's mother commented that her daughter was not as close to her paternal as her maternal grandmother.

> She is not as close as my mum is. But if they go up there on the weekend, either Saturday or Sunday – it's awkward in the week because of homework – so if she goes there on the weekend she will take them out. She will take them out for dinner.

Barbara (aged 9) explained that she saw her maternal grandparents nearly every day and saw her paternal grandparents on Sunday when her mother took them to their house. Barbara's father joined them later in the day when the family had lunch. Barbara made it clear that she loved all of her grandparents and looked forward to Sundays when she was taken to see her paternal grandparents.

Eleanor's mother commented on the secondary importance of paternal grandparents. However, she wanted her children to maintain contact and suggested that paternal grandparents in divorced families *should* continue to make frequent enquiries about their grandchildren. Her efforts to ensure that the grandparent–grandchild relationship survived the break-up had not been successful since these paternal grandparents had not reacted as she had expected.

> It's their [paternal grandparents'] choice but if you asked them, they would say it was my choice [for them not to see their grandchildren very often]. But, physically and emotionally, I couldn't keep going there any more because they made no effort to phone and see how the children were, to ring and say they'd like to see them, to invite us over.

Interestingly, some parents suspected that paternal grandparents were enthusiastic about their grandparenting role with their son's children until their own daughter had a baby and they were able to become 'main grandparents' themselves.

> She bonded very, very strongly with my first daughter and always thought of her as 'her favourite granddaughter', I think. Well, she's got two other grandchildren now and I think it's probably changed. We noticed the change – for the first two years she was all over my daughter and very lavish with her gifts and just wanted to be with her a lot. Then, her daughter had her baby and we watched the affection transfer which was interesting and then she started to compare them, in front of them, which wasn't too good. (Alan's mother talking about paternal grandmother's relationship with Alan's sister)

> But then when their daughters had children ... I always said, wait until their daughters have children and see how things change. (Linda's mother explaining her views on the paternal grandparents' priorities)

Lack of contact did not necessarily mean that grandchildren did not feel close.

> Kate was nine years old and had not seen her paternal grandparents (who lived more than 180 miles away) for over a year. They had kept in contact with her by sending letters and cards, and Kate explained that she was planning to ask her father if he would take her to see them.
>
> *Why are you going to ask if you can go and see them?*
>
> Because I do love them and I do want to go and see them and they are nice to me as well. (Kate, aged 9)
>
> Kate's mother reported that Kate was no longer close to her paternal grandparents. Kate, however, clearly felt emotionally close and wanted to see them again. She was therefore classified as one of the 16 grandchildren who felt close to her paternal grandparents.

Fathers looking after the children

There were 35 resident parents in our sample: only two were fathers. We wondered, in these two cases, whether the *paternal* grandparents were the main grandparents. Is it conceivable that the maternal grandmother could remain the dominant force when the father is the parent who has full-time care of the children? What happens when parents share care? Are maternal and paternal grandparents on a more equal footing or do maternal grandmothers remain the main grandparents whatever the circumstances? The answers to these questions seemed likely to shed new light on the reasons why research has identified grandmothers on the maternal side of the family as the 'main grandparents'. We had two families in which fathers shared childcare with their ex-wives. In both of these cases the parents lived near to the maternal and paternal grandparents.

Shared care and paternal grandparenting: Ingrid's family

Ingrid's parents live near to each other because her father, with help from his parents, bought a house only a few streets away from the family home. The maternal and the paternal grandparents' homes are also nearby. The parents share the task of caring for their three children and the arrangement helps Ingrid's father to cope with his job that involves shift work. It also allows Ingrid's mother to meet the demands of her job, which occasionally involves her being away from home overnight. Ingrid's father explained that he and his wife are still on friendly terms and cooperate well in making arrangements for the children.

Ingrid's paternal grandparents were also maternal grandparents with a daughter in an intact family. They had come to the conclusion that paternal grandparents *should* be less important. They explained why their rather limited contact with their grandchildren had not increased since their son's divorce.

The [maternal grandparents] came first.... They played the major role, and they still play the major role. We always understood that. We certainly would not begrudge them that – particularly because we play that same part in our daughter's children's lives. Then we come first. (Ingrid's paternal grandfather)

Their son and their grandchildren lived less than a mile away. Although their married daughter and their other grandchildren lived 80 miles away, it was these more distant grandchildren who were the main focus of their attention. It was a situation that Ingrid's father recognised. He also made reference to it to explain why his ex-parents-in-law (who lived two miles away) were much more involved with their grandchildren than his own parents.

It's like a lot of marriages. I mean, I was closer to my mother's mother than my father's mother. It seems that the same has carried on with us. I mean, there's no reason why they [the paternal grandparents] couldn't come up and see me and see the kids and they do if they haven't seen them for a while.

When asked why he did not take his children to see his parents more often, this father blamed the pressures that the shared care arrangements placed on him.

But, you know, by the time you've picked the kids up from school and taken them to every single club and all the rest of it and given them tea it's sort of seven o'clock. And perhaps, certainly during the winter, it's a time when they're looking to just sort of get their feet up and stick the telly on. I mean, I'm sure if you asked them [the paternal grandparents], they'd say, 'Yes, we'd like to see them more'. But, I mean, when you've got kids, it's just non-stop.

The maternal grandmother was close to her ex-son-in-law and saw her grandchildren five times every week. She expressed concern that the paternal grandparents were not more enthusiastic about grandparenting and more supportive of their son. The children's mother was equally critical.

Well, when we were married and we first had children, we were actually living on the same road as them. They very, very rarely ever called at our house, so if we didn't make an effort, the children would go two or three weeks without seeing them. And yet, with (ex-husband's) sister, they were always on call to go down ... to look after her children and were always very supportive of her children. But she [paternal grandmother] was very, very close to her daughter. (Ingrid's mother)

Ingrid, who was 11 years old, confirmed her mother's views.

They pick us up from school sometimes when we're at my dad's house. But, it's different for my [paternal grandparents] because I don't think they understood as much as my grandma and granddad [maternal grandparents] did, so there's not really a strong connection with them.

What was it they didn't understand?

I don't know. It's just that I think they sort of blamed it [the divorce] on – I don't know whether it was my mum or my dad. Probably my mum because they're my dad's parents. We're still close, yes, but not so close.

Shared care and paternal grandparenting: Debbie's family

Debbie's father also shared care of his children with his ex-wife. He hinted that he was closer to his parents around the time of his divorce but felt that when he had recovered from the initial shock, he and his children were no longer as involved as they had been initially. He spoke warmly about relationships with the maternal grandparents who were not only close to their grandchildren but also willing to help him whenever he asked.

So they [paternal grandparents] were very supportive throughout that period [around the time of the divorce] and I guess you become closer. But then, as time goes on, you gain more confidence and the hurt goes a little bit more and you pick yourself up and dust yourself down and move on – that's life. I suppose there were periods when they were particularly 'there'. I think it's difficult when you go through that sort of phase because you feel so isolated and even friends tend to be joint friends and you don't want people to be taking sides necessarily. It's having confidence in true friends and you need to establish who they are.

They [the children] are very, very close to [maternal grandparents]. And, equally, I think they've been extremely supportive, not only to my ex-wife's demands or expectations, but equally if I've had a problem. Obviously I don't see them [the maternal grandparents] as frequently but I think it's nice to know that you're able to pick up the phone to them if you need to.

These are unusual cases, not only because these fathers shared care with their ex-wives, but also because they both had good relationships with the maternal grandparents. In both cases, there is no obvious reason for a 'matrilineal advantage'; however, the maternal grandparents retained the primary position that they had enjoyed during the couples' marriages. Ingrid's paternal grandparents were especially interesting because of their suggestion that paternal grandparents should not 'begrudge' maternal grandparents their dominant position.

Resident fathers and paternal grandparenting

Two resident fathers, whose own mothers were alive and lived within a mile or two of their grandchildren, were interviewed. Belinda and her father had close relationships with Belinda's widowed paternal grandmother who was elderly and in poor health. The paternal grandmother had acted as a mother to her grandchildren when the mother – who was not interviewed – decided not to continue to look after her two young daughters. However, the case was not helpful in considering 'the main grandparent' because the paternal grandmother was the only living grandparent that the children had.

Robin's family was more interesting.

Despite having agreed to be interviewed, Robin's mother telephoned to withdraw. She had been the resident parent but her three children had decided one by one to live with their father because of their strained relationship with their mother's new partner. The grandchildren saw their paternal grandmother infrequently despite the fact that she had a car and lived in the same town about three miles away from her grandchildren. Robin's father reported that there had been no increase in their contact with the maternal grandmother since he had assumed responsibility for his three children. The interviews with this father and his mother provided some important insights.

No, my mother has only been here once since January. She is not interested in the children. The children will say, 'Why does nanna come here, smoke seven fags and then go away?'.

How often does she come to see them?

About three times a year.

Do you ever think about taking the children to her?

Not with my stepfather, no. (He explains that he does not like his widowed mother's husband.)

What about the other grandmother [maternal grandmother who lives 200 miles away]?

She is apparently moving down here this month sometime.

That's to be near her daughter?

Apparently, yes.

Although Robin's father was the resident parent, it was the maternal grandmother who was moving house to be nearer her daughter and grandchildren. The paternal grandmother who lived nearby was not an enthusiastic grandparent. Robin's maternal grandmother disliked her ex-son-in-law.

It would be interesting to find out whether this maternal grandmother's relationship with her ex-son-in-law improved after she moved house and whether or not she became the children's 'main grandparent'.

The evidence from the interviews in these four families needs to be treated cautiously. In one family, there were no maternal grandparents; exploration of the interview transcripts of the other three families revealed that all the paternal grandparents lived near to their grandchildren but were older than the maternal grandparents. It was not possible to be certain why these paternal grandparents appeared to be less involved with their grandchildren, and there were too few cases on which to base a general conclusion. However, the belief that a lack of opportunities for contact explains paternal grandparents' generally more distant relationships with their grandchildren was not confirmed by these interviews.

Differences between grandmothers and grandfathers

Mothers did not make a distinction between the quality of maternal grandmothers' and grandfathers' relationships with their grandchildren. However, this did not seem consistent with the comments that were made during the interview and, indeed, there were some striking inconsistencies. For example, a mother might spend some time explaining why her mother was more involved with her children than her father, but then assert that both of her parents were equally involved. The inconsistency was reconciled in some interviews in which mothers explained that their fathers might seem to be less affectionate whereas this was not actually true. In their accounts, the fact that grandfathers appeared to be relatively uninvolved hid the reality that they felt close to their grandchildren. This apparent contradiction could be explained by the commonly held view that men are less able to express their feelings. Men may also worry that they need to be careful about physical contact with adolescent granddaughters whose growing sexual awareness may make them less openly affectionate with their grandfathers. Clingempeel et al (1992) studied grandchildren's perceived closeness and involvement with grandparents at early and later stages of puberty and found that 'emotional distancing' occurred in granddaughter–grandfather relationships but not in the relationship between grandparents and grandsons.

Mothers did not want to believe that maternal grandmothers loved their grandchildren more than maternal grandfathers did. Tom's mother explained:

> They [men] might act differently because they're different people, but in terms of their affection or whatever towards the children, no, not at all. Mum might talk to them more, more detailed than father perhaps. I can't really read a lot into that. (Tom's mother)

> Grandma always wants to cuddle them and their grampa don't show that so much. He thinks it, but he don't show it. (Len's maternal grandmother)

Janet's maternal grandmother also said that she and her husband both liked to talk to their grandchildren on the telephone. She was contradicted by her husband, however.

> *Grandmother:* Yes, if it's the children [on the telephone], we have a chat with them.

> *Grandfather:* But, invariably, it's not me.

Although some grandparents expressed a belief in such gender stereotypes, others reported that they acted 'as a couple' when they were with their grandchildren, and so did not consider that there were any differences in their approach to grandparenting. Grandparents' comments, however, were not always entirely convincing.

For example, Karen's maternal grandfather said: "Our relationship with the children, our responses to the children, our dealings with the children tend to be more or less as one unit, together". However, he also noted, "I mean, she [his wife] sees them separately to me, but I don't normally see them separately to her".

Grandfathers occasionally exploded the myth that they were as involved with their grandchildren as their wives were. Some were willing to admit that they were not skilled at coping with their grandchildren.

> She has more time for them. She will get upset if they get hurt and puts up with them a lot more than I can. (Pauline's paternal grandfather)

Perceptions of differences between grandmothers and grandfathers

Parents, grandchildren and grandparents were asked to comment on any differences they perceived in grandmothers and grandfathers. Some grandparents did not believe that there were differences, and some parents confirmed the 'matrilineal advantage' hypothesis discussed earlier in this chapter. There were other explanations: it was suggested that gender differences in grandparenting might be explained in terms of grandparents' preferences for traditional gender roles, men's lack of competence in relationships with grandchildren, and women's dominance in the grandparenting role. It was not possible in this research to discover whether these explanations provided a valid account of grandparents' approaches to grandparenting. However, some illustrative quotations have been provided to give the flavour of parents' and grandparents' perceptions.

The importance of traditional gender roles

> It's two females, isn't it? If I had a grandson, it would be different. We'd go fishing. (Pat's paternal grandfather)

> I think she tried to teach her to knit once! When they were younger, she might have done a few more girly things with my daughter and my ex-father-in-law perhaps did more boy things with my son. (George's father)

> I'll be quite happy when any of the grandchildren come down there and pick up a spanner and tighten a few nuts. Do you know what I mean? (Karen's maternal grandfather)

Grandmothers are sort of fussy and grandfathers take you out on long walks and get you all muddy. They take you down the park and you come back plastered in mud. Where your grandmother wouldn't do that, she would take you down the park and sit you on the swings and make sure you didn't fall over so you wouldn't get dirty. I think they do things differently because they think, 'Oh she's a little girl and doesn't want to get dirty'. They think about it that way. But grandfathers don't think about it that way. They think, 'Oh don't worry!' and 'She'll be all right!' and that sort of thing. They do things differently. I don't know why, they just do. (Diana, aged 14, recalling the differences between her grandmother and her grandfather who died more than four years ago)

Grandfathers' confidence and competence in relationships with grandchildren

He [maternal grandfather] is not a family-orientated guy. If I actually said to him, 'What are all the children's names?', he'd struggle. (Valerie's mother)

He doesn't love them any the less. He just doesn't know how to do things as well as my mother. (Barbara's mother)

Although he loved him, he wouldn't do an awful lot with him; it wasn't his way – the old Victorian type man. (Robert's mother)

Grandmothers assumed a dominant presence in the grandparent role

She [maternal grandmother] is quite controlling. Men don't really think about things like that. I'm not being derogatory. They're just made differently. Most men wouldn't think, 'Oh, I must give my grandchildren a ring [that is, a telephone call]'. They would leave that to their wives to do, wouldn't they? (Jane's mother)

It's very difficult to tell because they [ex-husband's parents] always acted as a couple. They did have very different views of things but their front was always as a couple. He's actually much softer. My sense is that on his own he would probably have approached the children differently. (Peter's mother talking about her ex-husband's parents)

Children's views

Children commented on how much fun they had with their grandparents, whether or not they were bored, and which grandparents were strict and which were not. Some grandchildren clearly felt more comfortable with their grandmothers but others preferred their grandfathers' company. However, grandchildren did not usually make sharp distinctions between grandmothers and grandfathers (see also Spitze and Ward, 1998). Those who did point to differences did not give overwhelming support to grandmothers as their favourite grandparents and some especially enjoyed the company of their 'fun-seeking' grandfathers (see Chapter Four of this book).

Concluding comments

In this study, mothers and daughters usually had closer relationships than mothers and sons. After a divorce, the grandparents' positions continued to reflect this difference in the quality of men's and women's relationships with their parents. This might explain why some paternal grandparents said that they *expected* to play the minor role and why some mothers noted a cooling off in paternal grandparents' affections when their own daughter had her first child. Paternal grandparents' willingness to play the minor role and their shifting allegiances when they become maternal grandparents are topics that would benefit from further investigation with grandparents in intact as well as divorced families.

As Chapter Three noted, this study did not find that divorce itself was responsible for creating a different role for maternal grandparents: it simply had the effect of intensifying an existing hierarchy of grandparent importance. Our main conclusion, however, is that 'matrilineal advantage' may not simply be the result of maternal grandparents' enhanced opportunities for contact. A more detailed analysis would have to take account of differences between men's and women's relationships with their parents and cultural expectations about appropriate roles for maternal and paternal grandparents. The expectation that paternal grandparents in divorced families will assume a less significant role may not be imposed by mothers and maternal grandparents, but may be a perception that is also shared by paternal grandparents. Kornhaber (1996, p 40), however, has suggested that differences between grandparents are largely a matter of personal inclination or individual differences in personality.

> The Grandparent Study supports the observation of Robertson and Wood and Kivnick about the importance of personal factors in determining grandparenting and identity – factors that include temperament, individual experience, altruistic orientation and psychological style.

How can this be reconciled with the evidence of this study that grandparents' roles are determined to a significant degree by the position they hold in the family rather than their personal qualities? Maternal grandmothers are presumably as diverse in personality and temperament as any other category of family member. They may be highly significant *in the family group* by virtue of their mothering role but not necessarily pre-eminent in their grandchildren's eyes in their grandmothering role. Grandchildren, we discovered, do not always make the same distinctions between maternal and paternal grandparents as their mothers do, or between grandmothers and grandfathers. It is difficult, however, to separate children's enjoyment of paternal grandparents' company from the experience of seeing their father and enjoying the day with 'the other side' of the divorced family.

Therefore, we need to know much more about what grandparents do when they are with their grandchildren and what grandchildren and parents think about the time that they spend with their grandparents.

SEVEN

Grandparenting in divorced families: rights and policies

Grandparents and parental divorce

Research suggests that good quality contact between children in divorced families and their non-resident parent and grandparents is beneficial to their long-term adjustment (see Dunn and Deater-Deckard, 2001). There is a general conclusion that children's continuing contact with both parents is likely to be helpful in enabling them to avoid adverse reactions to their parents' divorce (Rodgers and Pryor, 1998). Marriage breakdown, however, can have negative effects on relationships between grandparents and grandchildren, and grandparents on the father's side of the family may see their grandchildren less frequently or, in some circumstances, lose touch with them entirely.

In their study of 86 members of the Grandparents' Federation in Britain, Drew and Smith (1999) asked whether grandparents, whose contact with their grandchildren had been lost as a result of divorce, were 'innocent victims' or 'agents in cross-generational family dysfunction'. Their study hypothesised that grandparents who had been deprived of contact with their grandchildren also had disturbed relationships with other family members. This might suggest, for example, that their difficulties with their sons and daughters-in-law were simply a symptom of wider personality and communication problems that made it difficult for them to form satisfactory relationships with others. The authors were unable to say whether grandparents were victims of divorce or "agents of their own misfortune" (Drew and Smith, 1999, p 210), but added that the general tenor of their findings pointed to them being "victims". However, grandparents who join a grandparent organisation are a special group in the sense that they are likely to have experienced conflict and to regard grandparenting as an important aspect of their lives. Our study, in contrast, investigated grandparenting that took place on a broad range of family circumstances and did not have a particular focus on families in conflict. Nevertheless, it did explore the feelings of a small number of grandparents who were deprived of contact and we comment (see Chapter Eleven) on their strategies for coping with the problem.

Cherlin and Furstenberg (1992), borrowing a phrase from Troll (1983), describe grandparents as the 'family watchdogs'. These authors explain that the extended family comes into its own at times of crisis and not at times of 'health and prosperity'.

The crisis of divorce calls into action the latent support network of the family; in which grandparents play a central part. In essence divorce recreates a functional role for grandparents, similar to the roles they had when higher parental mortality and lower standards of living necessitated more intergenerational assistance. (Cherlin and Furstenberg, 1992, p 197)

Cherlin and Furstenberg (1992) also appear to suggest that maternal grandparents, while regretting the circumstances of their children's divorce, secretly relish the opportunity for greater family involvement. Does a divorce in the family give the older generation a new sense of purpose or is the urge to get involved prompted by more primitive feelings about lineage and, if this is not too fanciful, an instinct to protect one's own genetic inheritance? Grandchildren – even those who have little or no relationship with their grandparents – may mean much more to grandparents than the friendly toddler who lives next door and is a frequent visitor. Although such feelings may be scarcely understood and difficult for most people to articulate, a greater understanding of how grandparents feel about their grandchildren might help to bring about changes in the way that grandparents are treated when couples divorce.

The legal position of grandparents

In many jurisdictions, grandparents have been given statutory rights to seek contact with their grandchildren. For example, in the US, all 50 states have passed legislation providing grandparents with a right of contact with their grandchildren. These statutes are often narrowly drawn, and many American states restrict grandparents' rights to cases of parental death, separation or divorce and the right to "sue for visitation" is not usually given to grandparents in intact families (Kornhaber, 1996, p 180). In some states where grandparents were able to seek contact in other circumstances, parents have campaigned successfully to have these laws rescinded on the grounds that they infringed their rights to bring up their children as they saw fit (Drew et al, 1998, p 475; Crook, 2001). In Europe, Germany and Italy have also granted rights to grandparents provided that contact is not likely to jeopardise the child's welfare. Werner (1991, p 74) explains that the effect of visitation rights legislation is to offer grandparents "an *independent* right of action that is not contingent on the rights already given to the child's parents".

The position is different in England and Wales. When child law was reformed by the 1989 Children Act, it was decided that parent–child relationships should be based on the exercise of responsibilities rather than rights. The express rights to seek contact that grandparents had previously enjoyed were accordingly repealed (Douglas and Lowe, 1990). Section 8 of the Act sets out the orders that are available to the court. These include a 'contact order' which requires the person with whom the child lives to allow the child to visit or otherwise contact the person named in the order and a 'residence order' which names the person or persons with whom the child will live. Under Section 10 of the Act, a parent (including an unmarried father with no parental responsibility), a guardian or anyone with whom the child has lived for a period of three years, is automatically entitled to apply for a residence or a contact order. Others, however, including grandparents, must first seek the court's leave to apply for an order. In deciding whether or not to grant leave, the court shall (under Section 10.9) have particular regard to:

1. the nature of the proposed application for the Section 8 order;
2. the applicant's connection with the child;
3. any risk there might be of that proposed application disrupting the child's life to such an extent that he or she would be harmed by it;
4. and where the child is being looked after by a local authority,
   - the authority's plans for the child's future;
   - the wishes and feelings of the child's parents.

The removal of the express right to seek 'access' under the old law was vigorously contested by grandparents' support groups during the passage of the Children Act. However, the Law Commission (1988, para 4.41) considered that the leave requirement in Section 10.9 would not be a significant hurdle for "close relatives such as grandparents" to overcome.

This two-stage process is controversial. We have argued elsewhere (Douglas and Ferguson, 2003) in favour of retaining the status quo since it acts as 'a filter' and protects families from being faced with unnecessary litigation. Legal proceedings can be entered into for misguided reasons. For some partisan paternal grandparents, for example, court action could represent an expression of loyalty to an aggrieved son. It might also be intended as a demonstration of disapproval of an ex-daughter-in-law that the grandparents hold responsible for the break-up of the family, rather than something in the best interests of the grandchildren.

Richards (2001), however, argued that it is unfair to make grandparents 'seek leave' before they can apply to the court for a contact order because they may suffer more anxiety and spend more money on legal proceedings than is strictly necessary. She advocated a special legal status being given to grandparents and her report recommended that they should *not* be required to seek leave when parents were absent or their application was supported by social services (Richards, 2001, p 107). However, she also identified cases of repeated applications by legally aided parents to reclaim children who were being brought up by their grandparents. She concluded that there is a need for greater scrutiny of applications because of the potentially damaging effects that legal proceedings often have.

Although Richards was discussing the plight of grandparent carers who were opposed by aggrieved parents, the same argument could be used to protect children from the disturbing effects of legal action by their aggrieved grandparents. Were grandparents able to obtain publicly funded legal assistance (legal aid) and had an automatic right to apply for contact, such proceedings could have an equally disruptive effect on the lives of parents and children. Richards' argument about the need for greater scrutiny of the merits of applications (which would need to be open and accountable) could be used to support the present 'two-stage process' which ensures that applications are examined before legal proceedings are begun in earnest.

Grandparents' rights

Now that the 1998 Human Rights Act has incorporated the European Convention on Human Rights into English law, grandparents could claim that they have 'rights' in respect of their grandchildren through their 'right to respect for family life' under Article 8 of the Convention. There is no definitive Strasbourg ruling on this matter, however. In *Marckx v Belgium* (1979, Series A, no 31), the European Court held that family life may include ties between grandparents and grandchildren, but the case concerned the state's recognition of the family ties of a child born outside marriage, rather than the content of those ties and their interaction with the rights of other family members (including the grandchild). In *Price v UK* (1982, 55 DR 224), the European Court of Human Rights considered that the blood tie by itself is insufficient to establish 'family life' between grandparents and grandchildren. More recently, in *L v Finland* (2000, 2 FLR 118), the Court took it more or less as read that the grandparental bond is not of the same significance as that between parent and child. Kaganas and Piper (2001) suggest further that, where there is parental opposition to grandparental involvement, the European Court is unlikely to uphold a complaint of breach because of its deference to the notion of parental authority.

It is, however, also important to recall that grandchildren (and parents too) have the same Article 8 rights. The existence of a 'family life' with a grandparent would need to be assessed from the children's and parents' perspective, and not just that of the grandparents. It would be necessary, therefore, in any given case, to turn to the content and nature of the ties that the grandparent (or grandchild) is asserting, to determine whether a right under Article 8 exists. Since the European Court has also affirmed on several occasions that the child's welfare will be the overriding consideration when determining claims under Article 8, this would be true even if the legislation were amended to provide grandparents with a right to seek contact without having to seek leave first. The grandparent organisations in the UK, unsurprisingly, have a different view of grandparenting to the one that is implicit in English law.

The Grandparents' Association

Grandparents caring full time for their grandchildren or those who have been excluded from seeing their grandchildren may turn for support to the Grandparents' Association. This is the largest grandparent organisation in the

UK, with around 900 members in England, Wales and Northern Ireland. It has a small group of members in the Republic of Ireland but no branches in Scotland where there are two quite separate and much smaller grandparent organisations.

Essentially, the association is a support service and a pressure group that campaigns to defend grandparents' interests. The membership has access to a telephone helpline (+44 (0)1279 444964), open meetings and conferences and a network of regional discussion groups where grandparents can seek advice and talk about the issues that concern them. It publishes a magazine, *Grandparent Times*, and has begun to organise playgroups for grandparents who look after their pre-school-age grandchildren while the parents are at work. About three quarters of the organisation's membership fall into the category of 'excluded grandparents', and around 60% of this rejected grandparent group have been denied contact as a result of parental separation. Not surprisingly, the Association's director reported that most are paternal grandparents who are seeking help to re-establish contact with their son's children. A substantial minority of grandparents have been denied access because they have quarrelled with a single parent or with both parents in an intact family. Family feuds, whether or not related to separation or divorce, are the main reason for grandparents being denied contact.

The Grandparents' Association recognises that quarrels are better solved with apologies and reconciliation than by legal means. Recognising the impossibility of mediation in which hostile resident parents are asked to meet face-to-face with angry grandparents, the Association is exploring the possibility of 'letter mediation'. This approach would allow trained staff to help grandparents to build bridges with the wider family in writing. However, the Grandparents' Association also recognises that legal action can be an important means of protecting grandparents' interests, and it strongly opposes the leave requirement in the 1989 Children Act, pointing out the additional legal costs involved and the paucity of publicly funded legal assistance. It strenuously rejects the argument that leave to apply for contact is 'a filter' that can prevent unnecessary litigation and protect the nuclear family from mischievous court action. It argues that few grandparents would seek legal advice and face the stress and the high costs of court action if they were not genuinely distressed by the loss of contact and determined to find a way of restoring their relationship with their grandchildren. In its opinion, the high cost is such an effective deterrent that it dissuades all but the most determined grandparents from seeking a contact order, possibly including many grandparents who would almost certainly be able to win their cases if they could find enough money. This controversial legal issue is not the only matter of public policy that is raised by grandparenting in divorced families. Grandparents are of interest to politicians and policy makers for a variety of other reasons.

Grandparenting and family policy initiatives

Two UK research projects have considered grandparents' roles and their relevance to public policy. In a study for the Family Rights Group, Richards (2001) focused mainly on grandparent carers who had a full-time responsibility for their grandchildren. However, she also investigated grandparents who looked after children so that their parents could go out to work. Arthur et al (2002) studied grandmothers' motivations for supporting their families and the negotiations that influenced the amount of financial and childcare support that grandparents were able and willing to provide. The 1998 Home Office consultation document, *Supporting families* (see Chapter One of this book), made recommendations about the support that families deserve from policies for health, welfare, employment, housing and education and also mentioned the role that grandparents might play. The document noted that grandparents are an important source of family support and assumed that they are often ready and willing to make sacrifices to help mothers to take up full-time employment or to provide support at moments of family crisis. It is a role that the government wants to encourage:

> The Government recognises the valuable role that grandparents and the extended family play in supporting parents and children and providing stability, alongside neighbours, friends and workmates. Most grandparents are already involved with the care of their grandchildren. A survey by Age Concern showed that 92 per cent of grandparents have regular contact with their grandchildren. They are the most important source of day-care of children: 47 per cent help look after their grandchildren. Most children see their grandparents as important figures in their lives. (Home Office 1998, section 1.59, p 14)

The document declared an intention to "help grandparents and older people to offer more support to families" (Home Office, 1998, Section 1.5, p 5) but there were few suggestions about how this might be achieved. Henricson (2003, p 2) believes that *Supporting families* indicates that the New Labour government is committed to "preserving family life as a very private affair". The consultation document contained a warning that service providers (social workers, healthcare professionals) could mistakenly marginalise grandparents; consequently, a number of consultation questions were highlighted. They were concerned with the effective use of grandparents in schools, the identification of 'best practice' guidelines for grandparents who are foster carers, how health visitors might be involved and the need to consider the wider family in the allocation of housing.

However, family policies aimed at supporting parents may mean that they need not rely exclusively on grandparents and other family members for support. For example, new measures that were put in place in April 2003 mean that traditional nuclear families, as well as families that have been restructured after separation or divorce, can be supported in their efforts to manage the demands of family life and employment more effectively. Any mother, father, guardian or foster parent with a child under the age of six who has been working for the same company for at least six months can now ask their employer for a more flexible work pattern. An employer who receives such a request has 28 days to respond by either granting the request or arranging a meeting to explain why the suggested arrangements are not workable (*The Guardian*, 5 April, 2003). If no suitable arrangement can be negotiated, the employer must give reasons in writing and give the employee an opportunity to appeal against the decision. Flexibility in employees' work conditions, at least for those parents with children under seven years of age, will make an important contribution to the quality of family life. Should employers detect increases in staff morale and productivity and reductions in absenteeism and staff turnover as a result of the introduction of flexible working, they may want to extend the provision to parents with older children.

Parenting has what Henricson (2003) calls a 'public face' because it has "deep-seated implications for society" (p 2). Grandparenting also has 'a public' as well as a 'private' face, and policy makers should be interested in grandparents and the roles they play in separated and divorced families. In her report for the Family Rights Group, Richards (2001) pointed to the adverse effects on the pension rights of grandparents who gave up work to look after their grandchildren. They had difficulty in claiming child benefit, tax credits and income support, and noted that delays were caused when the absent parent kept the child benefit book. Some were refused Working Families Tax Credit because they were not parents. Many were not given residence order allowances, which are discretionary payments and, as Richards discovered, those who did receive the payments discovered that these reduced their entitlement to other benefits. Grandparents might be living in poverty as a result of their decision to care for their grandchildren and many grandparents in these circumstances were receiving no financial help from social services. The system is in need of improvement, and there is a need for government intervention to provide consistency of treatment and avoid the 'postcode lottery' that is created when financial support is provided at the discretion of local authorities. However, the principle of supporting grandparents who assume full-time responsibility for children – perhaps preventing them from being taken into care – is not in doubt. Were grandparents acting as foster carers, it would not be unreasonable for them to receive the same recognition, support and the fostering allowances that other foster carers receive. In fact, a court has held (*R on the application of L and others v Manchester City Council; R on the application of R and another v Manchester City Council* (2001, EWHC admin 707) that it is unlawful to pay relatives less than other foster carers.

Concluding comments

The earlier chapters of this book have provided evidence to support the argument that no single view of grandparents can be said to provide an accurate picture. Rather, as we have seen, the grandparent role is interpreted in a wide variety of ways. It would be disappointing, however, to arrive at the conclusion that proposals, about the legal and family policy issues that have been introduced in this chapter, should simply 'take account' of this diversity: we rather suspected that before our study began. However, detailed information about the nature of grandparents' attitudes and beliefs can provide a useful basis on which to discuss these policy initiatives. Chapters Eight to Eleven now focus on grandparenting in divorced families and the policy implications of these four chapters are discussed in Chapter Twelve. In the next chapter, we begin with an exploration of 'non-communication' in divorced families.

EIGHT

Communicating in divorced families

Introduction

This chapter explores how, and to what extent, the three generations in our group of divorced families communicated with each other about marriage breakdown and its consequences. First, it looks at the way that parents warned their own parents about their impending separation, and then investigates what the grandchildren told their mothers, fathers and grandparents about their relationships with the 'other side' of their divided families. The chapter also investigates whether or not children were used as conduits for the flow of information between the two sides of the divorced family.

Telling grandparents about the planned separation

Although grandparents were not asked directly when and how they were told about the breakdown of their child's marriage, the interview guide included questions about their relationships with grandchildren before and after the separation. Almost half the grandparents interviewed mentioned their surprise at learning of their child's separation. It was common for parents to hide their marriage problems from their own parents and the news of the separation often came as a shock to grandparents. Parents admitted that they were reluctant to take grandparents into their confidence, but their explanations made it clear that this was neither symptomatic of a lack of affection nor a failure to anticipate the likely effects of their separation on the wider family. A rather similar conclusion, it may be recalled, was made as a result of the investigation of children's reluctance to confide in their grandparents when they felt upset or worried about family break-up (see Chapter Three).

The deliberate concealment of problems might be interpreted as evidence that parents did not consider grandparents to be involved. However, divorced couples were also concerned about disappointing their parents; they were worried about invoking their displeasure and anxious to protect them from the pain of their divorce – feelings that are characteristic of many parent–child relationships. The interview data revealed that most mothers had worried needlessly and were pleasantly surprised by their parents' reactions to being told that the marriage had ended. For example, Alfie's mother recalled:

Really, my parents could have said to me, 'What are you doing, splitting up? This is so wrong! Don't be ridiculous! For goodness sake, pull yourself together!' . But they listened to what I had to say. And, rightly or wrongly, they love me and they told me so.

Alan's maternal grandmother explained that their daughter had concealed her marriage problems from her and her late husband, and they were surprised when she told them that she had left her husband. When Alan's mother was interviewed, she explained that she had left home with "a briefcase" and that her parents were "devastated" by her announcement that she was leaving her husband.

Absolutely devastated, because they had no idea what was going on. I'd put it off for about five years. I hadn't left for five years because I didn't actually want to upset them. They've got very strong religious views and I just felt, well this is the worst scenario that they could possibly have and I didn't want to upset them. But in the end it got so I couldn't stay [with her husband]. They were upset but they were very, very supportive.

Alan's grandmother confirmed this version of events but gave no hint of the 'devastation' that her daughter had described.

We were actually surprised ... because she kept it hidden very well. She did not want us to know things and we just did not realise how unhappy she was.

Kate's mother commented, "I hid the bad side of my marriage from them" and added, "When I decided to be straight and honest with them I think I gained respect". She attributed her new, improved relationship with her parents to their appreciation of her "suffering" and believed that "We are a much tighter bond now".

However, the fact that parents often found it difficult to tell their own parents about their marriage breakdown also caused problems. A father clumsily informed all of his children's grandparents at his child's birthday party that he and his wife intended to separate. This made his parents and the maternal grandparents angry at his insensitivity. His wife described the paternal grandparents' shocked and angry reaction.

Another mother felt that the fact that she had not told her mother herself had backfired on her.

We phoned my mother to inform her of us divorcing. I actually didn't, my ex-husband did, and it was a case of instead of saying, 'Look we are just not getting on, we're going to divorce', it was, 'She's found another man, but I can't prove it'. (Frank's mother)

It is not only mothers who cannot or do not tell their parents. Eleanor's father had not told his parents about the separation and they only discovered the truth when their daughter-in-law telephoned them.

> I phoned them [her parents-in-law] and said, 'I don't know if you know but C [ex-husband] has actually left me'. And they didn't know! He hadn't told them! So I told them the facts and they were horrified. And they rang back and said, 'If there's anything we can do, you've only got to say blah, blah, blah'. But it takes quite a brave person to say, 'Yes, I need help' – especially in a situation like that.

Eleanor's maternal grandmother pointed to the part that grandparents play in encouraging their divorced sons and daughters to exhibit dependency. Grandparents, she reasoned, step in for the sake of their grandchildren and can be said, therefore, to have volunteered for their 'second parenthood'.

Parents' fears about causing distress to their own parents were occasionally justified. Some grandparents found it painful talking about the moment when they first realised that their child's marriage had ended.

> I would say she hid it for about nine months to a year, maybe, and then we were out one day and she said that they were going to separate and so I was numb for a few days and then I couldn't stop crying. But that's just me, because it is very difficult to explain. Your world falls apart when you think that your children are not happy. (Ingrid's maternal grandmother)

A trouble shared

These examples illustrate some of the worries that divorced couples had about upsetting their own parents and the awkwardness that parents felt about re-establishing contact with parents-in-law, including those who made gestures of friendship towards them. Evidence from our study was that sons did not usually tell their mothers about their extra-marital affairs for understandable reasons. Paternal grandmothers, in particular, were sometimes enraged when they felt that their son had been responsible for the separation and divorce.

In general, grandparents did not blame their adult children for concealing their problems and there was no evidence that the middle generation's attempts to keep things from their own parents affected relationships in the wider family. In cases where grandparents were upset at being excluded, their anger was short-lived and the relationship was unaffected in the long run.

> Carl's maternal grandparents remained on good terms with both of his parents. Their grandchildren (aged 16 and 17) had lived with their father in the marital home in the early months of the separation but had since decided to live with their mother. This

maternal grandmother was initially disappointed that her daughter had kept her marriage problems from her.

> I was upset because she hadn't come to me, because we've always had that mother–daughter relationship. I said to her, 'Why didn't you come and tell me? Why didn't you come and talk to me?'. I would have been ready to listen to her. She said, 'I didn't like to. I was afraid of what you'd say'. And I said, 'Well, I'm not that much of an ogre. I'd have thought you'd have known me by now'. I think she wanted to tell me but she was so upset. But I said I was here for her, like, and gave her cuddles, and talked to her and I said to her, 'You've just got to get on with your life now'. But I think she was more worried about her dad than she was me, really.

Carl's mother, as her own mother had guessed, had hidden her marriage problems from her parents because, as she explained in her interview, "I never really wanted to shatter my dad's dreams". She commented:

> But I don't know whether I did shatter my dad's dreams. I asked Denise [Carl's 17-year-old sister] because my dad is still a bit edgy. My dad always says to me, 'Don't ever forget, I love you'. I said to Denise the other night, 'I don't know why he says that in such a way'. She said, 'Do you think it's because you didn't go to him, didn't tell him what was happening and why it was happening?'.

This mother and her parents provided a good example of the rather opaque communications that were sometimes used between close family members. Her remarks about 'shattering her father's dreams' were a further illustration of a point made earlier. Many parents in this study appeared to exhibit behaviour that suggested a return to childhood dependency. It was interesting that Carl's mother returned to this parent–child relationship at a point in her life when, as she explained, her parents' help had become important to her and her children. Brown and Day-Sclater (1999, p 149), in their discussion of the psychodynamics of divorce, note that "the family continues to exert an emotional hold over us long after we have ceased to feel dependent upon it". Furthermore, adults appear to display submissive, childlike behaviour when they are most in need of their parents' help.

One of the most surprising pieces of evidence was provided by Norman's maternal grandparents who were interviewed at their daughter's home. These grandparents knew that their daughter had separated from her husband, but the appointment with a member of the research team had prompted their daughter to tell them, on the morning of the interview, that she had divorced her husband. Like other grandparents in this study, news of the problems in the marriage and the decision to separate had come "as a complete surprise". These grandparents had wondered if their daughter was divorced, but had not liked to ask. Their daughter had not volunteered the information and, as they explained, they had not asked questions. This was in a family in which the maternal grandparents, their daughter and their grandchild reported that they had close and loving relationships. It was a graphic example of the way that families avoided awkward subjects and direct communication about painful issues. Such matters were intended to be 'understood' despite the fact that they had never been communicated.

In their explanation of 'systems theory' and its application to family research, Klein and White (1996, pp 149-77) provide an example of a wife whose husband had been giving her roses for 10 years. She did not like roses and blamed her husband for not being more sensitive and for his failure to pick up the subtle cues that would have told him that she liked 'the thought', but not the roses. She felt that, after 10 years of marriage, he ought to have known her better. In this case the couple's interaction system was damaging their relationship and we might well wonder why the wife did not tell her husband about her taste in flowers. The answer is that the communication was a difficult one and she hoped that her behaviour would have given enough information for her husband to understand her feelings without being told.

Parents and grandparents, in this study, provided similar evidence of these rather obscure communications. However, it was not generally the case that their adult children hid their unhappy relationships from their parents, but hoped that they might be sensitive enough to pick up the non-verbal cues. Rather, they seemed to be at pains to conceal the information for as long as possible in order to delay the moment when news of the break-up would kindle distress and cause their own guilty feelings about the failure of their marriage to surface. Although divorce may be relatively free of stigma and increasingly common, the process of family break-up was so painful for many of the individuals in this study that 'non-communication' became a coping mechanism. Parents did not want to burden their own parents with their marriage problems and they believed (initially at least) that 'a trouble shared was a trouble doubled'. This changed soon after the separation when mothers often turned to their parents to provide extra financial, childcare and emotional support, and fathers often asked their parents for temporary accommodation, financial support or help on the days when they were responsible for the children.

The 'other side' of the divorced family

Close families, it seemed, did not want to talk about matters that were awkward to broach, difficult to explain or likely to cause embarrassment and distress to children and other family members. Ann's mother, for example, explained that her good relationships with her ex parents-in-law depended on a shared resolve *not* to discuss past events.

> I think I get on pretty well with them really. We very rarely talk about [ex-husband] or anything like that. They are very discreet. They would never say anything to upset me and they wouldn't have ever done anyway, before we broke

up.... They keep things pretty much close to their chests to keep equilibrium, I suppose. That hasn't changed. They were like that before.

The weight of evidence from the interviews suggested that parents and grandparents did not ask questions about children's life with the other side of the divorced family. The interview data did not indicate that children were asked by grandparents to act as 'go-betweens'; neither, apparently, were they pressed much for information about their resident or non-resident parents and grandparents. This finding is contrary to other studies (Douglas et al, 2000). However, it seems that children may not have been questioned by their mothers about their relationships and activities with their paternal grandparents. Nor were they likely to be probed by their grandparents about their relationships and activities with their other parent. Parents who asked their children questions about their ex-spouse were given little or no information. Children made it clear to parents and grandparents alike that they were not willing to be questioned about these things, especially where this would appear to be testing the children's loyalty to the other side of their divorced family. Indeed, we found that children as young as eight years of age remained loyal to both their parents and maintained discretion when talking to their families.

> They never really say one way or the other. They just say we've been to grampy's [paternal grandfather]. I get no feedback. I wonder why that is? They don't talk about the visit. Just that they have been there and that's it. I've really no idea of what goes on down there as such. (Marion's mother taking about Marion, aged 13, and her seven-year-old sister)

> I think really they [parents] would have liked for him to have come out with a lot more, but Carl don't. He keeps it inside of him. (Carl's maternal grandmother discussing her grandson's refusal to talk about his visits to his father)

Johnston and Campbell (1988), who studied families in which the parents' contact with children had become a source of conflict resulting in legal proceedings, made similar findings. Their study described children's need to retain neutrality and cope with the loyalty conflicts they encountered when their parents pressed them to take sides.

Eleanor's mother and maternal grandmother had both noted that Eleanor did not disclose any information about her visits to her father and paternal grandparents.

> What sort of things do they do with your ex-husband's parents?

> I don't really know.

> Don't they talk about it when they have been over there?

You know I say something like, 'What did you do?'. They will say, 'Nothing really'. The contact she has with them [paternal grandparents] is when she's with her dad. I don't know about it. She doesn't tell me anything about it. (Eleanor's mother)

Eleanor's maternal grandmother also noted that Eleanor did not talk about her father and believed that her grandchild was 'protecting' her relationships.

Do the children ever express any feelings to you about their father?

No, they're very guarded about that always. They hardly will ever tell us anything about it.

Edward was one of the children who felt that visits to grandparents were 'boring'. His mother claimed to know almost nothing about her children's relationship with their paternal grandparents and had realised that her children did not like being questioned about their regular visits to see their father.

Well, I think he takes them over there [to the paternal grandparents' house] sometimes. I don't really know the frequency of it but I know they do go over there sometimes. Well, they don't talk about it! They come back and I say to them, 'What have you done this weekend?', and they say, 'We went to nanny and grandpa yesterday'.

Tom, aged eight, enjoyed his regular visits to his grandparents' homes. Like other children, he was willing to talk to a researcher about his experiences but was apparently unwilling to talk to his parents about his relationships with the 'other side' of his divorced family. Tom's father knew little about his children's relationship with their maternal grandparents.

Do the children like going to see [maternal grandparents]?

I don't know.

It's not something you talk about?

Not really. I've no reason to discuss it. The kids would say to me if they didn't like it.

Norman's maternal grandparents also said that they knew little about the 'other side' of the family. They had a close relationship with their grandson but were surprised that they could not persuade Norman (aged 10) to tell them anything about his telephone calls to his father whom he rarely saw.

Grandmother: One thing he would not talk about is his dad, not at all.

Grandfather: He would feel he was being disloyal.

Grandmother: Yes. I will say to him, 'Have you spoken to dad today?', and all he'll say is, 'Yes'. Sometimes if I am there, I answer the phone and I shout to him that it's his dad. He will talk to him and then I ask what he had to say. He would say, 'Nothing'.

Norman's maternal grandmother continued to ask questions but her husband clearly understood why Norman was unlikely to answer them. For children, being discreet, respecting boundaries and avoiding questions that threatened to compromise their neutrality or test their loyalty to one of their parents, seemed to be part of the experience of living in a divorced family.

One mother who sensed that her child was being tactful and telling her what she wanted to hear, made light of it and teased her affectionately.

When you're cuddling up in bed at night and we have issues about her not having time to do things when she goes to D's [her father's house] and she says, 'I just get a bit bored when I go there'. And she did come out and say, 'I don't like going there', and I must admit, I laughed and said, 'Well, that's not true, is it?', and she grinned. (Ann's mother)

These children in divorced families appear to have learned the value of non-communication and its contribution to harmony. Older children might have arrived at a conscious decision to keep the two parts of their lives separate. Younger children may have been instructed not to give information to the 'other' side of the family.

At Christmas time I asked the little girl, I said what did you have for Christmas then and she said I'm not allowed to tell you nan, so I just left it at that. (Pauline's paternal grandmother)

Another possible reason for children's non-communication is that they have learned to be discreet because of their parents' and grandparents' apparent lack of curiosity. When family members did not ask, because they felt that it was wrong to intrude, children may have concluded that they should not tell. In some cases, parents' and grandparents' refusal to pry into grandchildren's relationships with the other side of the divorced family may have helped to preserve a stable and harmonious set of conditions in which arrangement for contact could be made.

Learning discretion, avoiding causing hurt to parents and grandparents and recognising the sensitivity of their situation might also have been skills that the children acquired gradually as their parents' marital problems developed. Their parents' separation and divorce were the culmination of a longer process of

---

family breakdown, which might well have taught children to be more cautious and sensitive in their dealings with their families. In relation to this, Weiss (1979) has commented on the 'maturity demands' that are placed on adolescent children in single-parent families. Wallerstein and Kelly (1980, p 83) have claimed: "one potential major impact of divorce is either to drive adolescent development forward at a greatly accelerated tempo, or bring it to a grinding halt".

Concluding comments

Parents frequently hid their family problems from their own parents and postponed the announcement that they were separating from their spouse for as long as possible. Grandparents were usually shocked when they were told that their child had separated and was planning to divorce. Often, close family members did not ask questions or volunteer information about sensitive topics. Avoidance of opportunities to talk things over was so common that 'the norm of non-communication' might arguably join the norms of 'non-interference' (to which it is closely related) and 'obligation' (see Aldous, 1995) in defining the rules which families apply to the management of their day-to-day affairs.

Should we feel reassured that family members react in these difficult circumstances with discretion and sensitivity? Or should we wish that families communicated clearly enough to agree aims, avoid confusion (Olson et al, 1989) and come to an understanding of the submerged ideologies and hidden agendas (Street, 1997) that affect family life?

Yalom (1995) has compiled a list of curative factors that members of counselling groups believed were the most significant. The second and third items on Yalom's list were "being able to say what was bothering me rather than holding it all in" and "other group members telling me honestly what they think of me" (p 82). It is not immediately obvious, however, that this advice about honesty and openness should apply without qualification to parents, grandparents or children in divorced families.

A lack of 'emotional openness' is presented as an unfortunate characteristic of human interaction in the counselling literature (Komiya et al, 2000). Lee and Liu (2001) make a distinction between direct coping (active management, seeking out advice and support) and indirect coping (passive avoidance and withdrawal) in family conflict. These authors conclude that strategies that led to family members' refusing to be open with one another caused greater anxiety and distress. In the introduction to their article, however, they advance an argument that is more in tune with the approach to family communications that was taken by the parents, children and grandparents who took part in this study:

> In some contexts, such as within families and collectivist milieus, efforts to actively remove the stressful demand may not be possible, and more indirect coping may be more appropriate. (Lee and Liu, 2001, p 411)

It is tempting for policy makers and those who offer advice to families to wonder how family communication about divorce could be improved. Ferri and Smith (1996) studied parenting in the 1990s and concluded that there was a need to give family life a central place in the National Curriculum so that communication and relationship skills could be improved. The authors wanted to see a "negotiated acceptance of each other's experiences, expectations and aspirations" (p 50). Communication – and non-communication – between parents, children and grandchildren within divorced families and across the family divide is a topic that should, in our view, be given more attention because of its implications for professionals who are involved in supporting families when parents divorce. It is an issue that is discussed in the final chapter, which looks at some of the policy implications of our findings.

NINE

Taking sides

Introduction

Following parental separation and divorce, grandparents in our study usually sympathised with their adult child and criticised the behaviour of their ex-son or ex-daughter-in-law. However, this was not the only strategy and, although it is recognised that divorce is a difficult process, some couples appeared to achieve reasonably harmonious arrangements and a minority of grandparents demonstrated that their non-partisan approach could also make a contribution to harmony. Most, however, did not think about the longer-term implications of their relationships with an ex-child-in-law. They were often angry and some were bitterly partisan in their feelings. Some grandparents took sides after the break-up and continued to harbour strong feelings of resentment for their sons or daughters-in-law long after their child's marriage had ended. Parents often reported that their own parents had ceased contact with their ex-spouse because they held him or her responsible for the failure of the marriage. This was often presented as a natural feeling and one that might reasonably be expected of grandparents in a divorced family.

Grandparents' partisan feelings

Twenty-five grandparenting couples and 11 lone grandparents in 30 different families were interviewed in the course of the research. There were 21 interviews with maternal grandparents and 15 with paternal grandparents. Five maternal and two paternal grandparents took an apparently neutral stance when asked about their relationship with their ex-child-in-law. They said that they were 'civil' and 'polite' to their child's ex-spouse or explained that there was 'no contact but no animosity'. In nine grandparent interviews (five with maternal and four with paternal grandparents) it was clear that they had retained friendly relationships with their divorced child's ex-spouse. However, more than half of our grandparents (11 maternal and 9 paternal) expressed resentment.

Grandparents' resentment

Ann's parents and maternal and paternal grandparents were all interviewed. Ann is eight years old and has a three-year-old brother. Ann has learning difficulties (this aspect of her relationship with her grandparents was discussed in Chapter Four of this book).

Ann's parents divorced two years ago and Ann's father had a new partner. Ann's mother had maintained friendly relationships with the paternal grandparents but the maternal grandparents were angry with their ex-son-in-law. Ann's mother took Ann and her brother to see her ex-husband's parents almost every week. Ann's father had moved to a new home about 120 miles away and, in the early months of the separation, had seen his children infrequently. Now, however, he had agreed to see them every other weekend. The maternal grandparents resented the weekends that their grandchildren spent with their father and his parents:

> The fortnight business only started six months ago. I'm only in agreement with it in as much as it gives our daughter a break.

The maternal grandmother complained that 'it was not fair' that the paternal grandparents saw more of the children than they did and commented that Ann's younger brother would probably grow up thinking that his father was 'wonderful'. She added:

> I know they [grandchildren] have to have some relationship with their father but I don't think he deserves to see them. That sounds awful but that's what I feel.

The interview illustrated the strength of grandparents' partisan feelings and their durability. It raised the possibility that grandparents might harbour feelings of jealousy about the contact that grandparents on the other side of the divorced family have with their grandchildren.

Janet's maternal grandparents did not like Janet's father. They had opposed the marriage from the outset and had let their daughter know that they disapproved of her choice of husband. They had made a last-minute attempt to persuade her not to marry him, but she ignored their pleas. The case is interesting because, as Janet's maternal grandmother explained, her first reaction on hearing about the break-up was a feeling of relief that her daughter had freed herself from a husband that she had never liked. Her second thought was one of concern for her grandchildren whose father had left home. The immediate focus of these grandparents' attention was their adult child rather than their grandchildren.

> At the time for me, it was sheer relief when she said they'd split. All I felt was relief. And then, of course, all the other feelings come in don't they? About the [grand]children. (Janet's maternal grandmother)

Janet (aged nine) refused to see her father, although her younger brother spent every Saturday afternoon with him. Janet's mother described the anguish that both her children had felt when their father left the family home to stay with his parents a little over two years ago. Janet's maternal grandparents were angry:

> We would have liked the bugger to have gone and disappeared off the face of the earth. Down a pit. Right? And, if any arrangement could have been made to make that happen we would have supported that. (Janet's maternal grandfather)
>
> And the feeling hasn't diminished one iota in the years that they have been divorced. Not with me anyway. In fact, it's getting stronger. (Janet's maternal grandmother supporting her husband's views)

The grandparents who made the most negative comments about their ex-sons and daughters-in-law were usually those whose adult children had divorced only two years ago. Grandparents whose children had been divorced in 1997 were usually more restrained; perhaps because time had blunted their anger and provided a different sense of proportion. This was not always the case, however, and Marion's maternal grandparents who are discussed below, demonstrated that some grandparents' bitterly partisan feelings could be detected when the couple had been divorced for four years or more.

A normal hostility?

Parents often suggested that taking sides was a predictable response. They appeared to believe that grandparents' partisan behaviour was 'natural' and should be seen as an inevitable consequence of their divorce.

> It's quite natural. He's their son and it is understandable, as with most parents, that they are going to be there for him. (Annabel's mother)

Ingrid's parents had divorced amicably and her father had remained close to Ingrid's maternal grandparents. However, the paternal grandparents blamed Ingrid's mother for the divorce and had severed their relationship with her. Ingrid's father described the day that he had told his parents that he and his wife had separated and planned to divorce.

> You know my old man said, 'Right that's it, she's not coming in this house again'. And I said, 'Hang on! I haven't told you why we are getting divorced!'. That was his sort of reaction. My parents just, both of them if you like, turned around and they totally blamed [ex-wife] even though I was there trying to say, well hang on, this was my bit. This is the reason why she went off me. Well, that was sort of totally dismissed. 'You're my son. She shouldn't upset my son'.

Fathers were usually left in no doubt about their ex-parents-in-law's feelings. Martin's father reported that his ex-mother-in-law refused to speak to him.

> She won't speak to me. Once she knows it's me, the phone is down.

Robin's maternal grandmother had also let her ex-son-in-law know that she blamed him for the break-up of the family.

> See, I am the big 'baddie' in all of this. I was the one who drove my wife away. I was a drunken abusive alcoholic who didn't want to work. That's according to my mother-in-law. I was also a common little Welshman with tattoos. (Robin's father)

Some fathers would only joke about their relationship with their ex-wife's parents but nevertheless made it clear that their ex-parents-in-law had turned against them.

> We don't talk. In fact, if I was walking across the street one day and he [maternal grandfather] was in a car, he'd probably run me over. (Brian's father)

Among the 16 fathers who were interviewed, one had no ex-parents-in-law; two reported that they had had a difficult relationship with their ex-parents-in-law that was now improving; four had friendly relationships; and nine had poor relationships. Each of these fathers had things to say about their post-divorce relationships with their ex-parents-in-law. Their children's grandparents had not become an irrelevance as a result of the divorce and there was a sense that parents were still involved in, or at least not completely free from, emotional entanglements with the wider family.

Accounting for partisan behaviour

Pearlin (1982), in a study of life-course transitions, found that divorced people were not so much distressed by the divorce per se as by the difficulties of adjusting to life as a single person. He went on to claim:

> Thus among the divorced people whose circumstances are relatively benign, judged especially by the level of their economic resources, there is virtually no emotional distress associated with divorce; and among those who have gone through the same marital disruption but who have ended up in difficult and demanding economic straits, distress is likely to be intense. (Pearlin, 1982, pp 66-7)

For some grandparents, the divorce of their son or daughter was perceived as presenting a significant threat. It brought an unwelcome intensification of their childcare obligations and disrupted the anticipated pattern of their lives. Pearlin's thesis suggests that an unwelcome disruption to the course of life rather than any direct consequences of the divorce itself might provide a better explanation for the ferociousness of some grandparents' comments. It may help to explain why some grandparents appeared to be angrier than their own son or daughter and had more acrimonious relationships with their child's ex-spouse than the divorced couple had with each other. Eleanor's maternal grandparents, for example, had enjoyed a good relationship with their son-in-law when the couple was married but now felt bitter about the divorce and had severed all connections with him. Their daughter had maintained a good relationship with her ex-husband but her relationship with the paternal grandparents had become unfriendly since the divorce. When Eleanor's mother was asked about her relationship with her ex-husband, she spoke much more positively about him than about her ex-parents-in-law.

> *Do you have much contact with him [ex-husband]?*
>
> Yeah. We're quite good friends. I see him every other weekend when the children go there. (Eleanor's mother)
>
> *What about your parents-in-law? How often do you see them?*
>
> I don't see them any more.
>
> *How far away are they?*
>
> Oh, they're ever such a long way away [said sarcastically]. About nine miles. I've just about had enough of them. (Eleanor's mother)

Ann's mother hinted that her parents' strongly partisan feelings towards her ex-husband had had some negative effects on her own relationship with her parents.

> Obviously they're very anti-him anyway. I don't want to be dragged down into what's right and wrong. You just have to get on with it. Perhaps they would be upset by me saying this, but I don't necessarily go to them if I'm feeling down or miserable. I wouldn't say that means that we don't have a close relationship. I think we do.

Ann's maternal grandparents had continued to harbour acrimonious thoughts long after the hostility between husband and wife had abated, and this, it seems, had negative effects on their relationship with their divorced daughter.

The problem of maintaining good relationships

Five sets of *paternal* grandparents (four of whom had close relationships with their daughters-in-law when their sons were married) maintained good relationships after the divorce. (The reasons why they did so are discussed in the next chapter.) Some *maternal* grandparents maintained good relationships with their ex-sons-in-law. Ingrid's and Carl's maternal grandparents, for example, had close relationships with their ex-sons-in-law. Ingrid's parents shared care of their children and these maternal grandparents' close relationship with their ex-son-in-law enabled them to maximise their contact with their grandchildren. Ingrid's maternal grandmother explained her feelings:

> He is still the father of our grandchildren and that will never change. Our relationship would never change even if [ex-son-in-law] was to blame, because at the end of the day we have got these three children who idolise their dad and we wouldn't jeopardise that at all.

Carl's maternal grandparents' relationship with their ex-son-in-law can only be explained in terms of an affection that was able to withstand the impact of the divorce. They said that they had refused to apportion blame and the divorce, they claimed, had had no effect on their relationship with Carl's father.

> *Maternal grandmother:* I could have turned round and said to him, 'You hurt her. That's it!', and not have bothered with him no more. But I couldn't do that to him.... I suppose there's a lot of people thinking, 'Fancy being friendly with your ex-son-in-law!'.

> *Maternal grandfather:* He's not a son-in-law. He's a son, isn't he?

Both Carl's and Ingrid's maternal grandparents had known their ex-sons-in-law since they were adolescents. But other close relationships between maternal grandparents and their sons and daughters-in-law did not survive the divorce and often led to a sense of loss. Mothers were very often sorry to lose their friendship with their ex-husband's parents and expressed regret when family divisions meant that their children were deprived of regular contact with their paternal grandparents. They claimed that they wanted to re-establish good relationships but hesitated to make the first approach and contact was lost. Alfie's paternal grandparents had severed contact with his mother. She had tried, in a small gesture of friendship, to heal the rift but discovered that it was now too late to restore the relationship.

> I did send a couple of envelopes with photographs in, a long time ago. And then word came back via the children. They just said, 'Thank you very much'.... I got on all right with them. It's a shame, isn't it? But there you are. It's gone too far. I just could not pop over now or even phone up. I think they would feel terribly, terribly uncomfortable with it now. (Alfie's mother)

Edward's mother also regretted that she had lost contact with her ex-parents-in-law but felt aggrieved that they had not acknowledged that their son's adultery had caused his marriage to end.

> I would like it very, very much if we could have remained close. I am not saying that I want them to hate their son or cast him from their lives but to purely accept that he has done something very, very wrong. He has done something

bad to his family. They should still love him but should have still welcomed me and my children as part of their family. This didn't happen.

Two years ago, Kate's mother decided to travel from Wales to the south east of England and stay in a hotel so that her children could renew their acquaintance with the paternal grandparents whom they had not seen for over two years. Since that visit, there had been no more meetings and she reflected ruefully that she had found it harder to leave her ex-mother-in-law than to leave her husband. She had continued to try to renew her relationship with her ex-parents-in-law but realised that her attentions were "rubbing salt in the wounds" and that it was time to "stand back and let the wounds heal". There had been no more contact but Kate's mother still regretted the loss of a close friendship.

Some demonstration of hostility was the expected response and grandparents who did not feel angry were aware that they were behaving in unexpected ways. Their adult children were also likely to be disappointed or confused by non-partisan behaviour.

> Oh, I hated it to begin with. I felt that my parents should support me completely. But again I had to sit back and decide what was best for the children. And, again, I think it's best for the children if all these people that they separately love are nice to each other.... I didn't let them know that I didn't like it because that would have been unfair to them. It would have put them in an awkward situation. But, I would say I've only come to terms with it myself over the last few months. (Ingrid's mother)

Earlier it was noted that the most partisan grandparents were those in the second group whose sons and daughters had divorced less than two years ago. Ingrid's mother was also suggesting that families learn to come to terms with divorce and its aftermath. The impact of divorce cannot be judged just in the short term and this fact points again to the importance of studying the impact of divorce over time and not relying on an immediate 'snapshot' to provide information about its effects on the wider family (see Chapter Two).

The origins of partisan behaviour

Post-divorce hostilities were perceived as a radical change of a previously affectionate relationship in six of the 20 interviews with grandparents who admitted to being partisan in their behaviour. Marion's grandparents, for example, commented that they used to get on "like a house on fire" with their son-in-law but they were unable to forgive him for the adulterous relationship that had ended their daughter's marriage. Some four years after the divorce, Marion's grandmother still felt angry and there was a sharp contrast between the feelings she expressed and her memories of the earlier relationship with her ex-son-in-law.

He was in my house from the time he was 14. Breakfast, dinner, tea and supper when they were home from school. I knew where they were. So she's never had any other boyfriend. So really, he was like a son to me.

She went on to explain contemptuously that she had seen her ex-son-in-law "with his floozy" in town but when he noticed her he "hid" behind the supermarket shelves.

Fourteen of the 36 grandparents claimed that they had never felt a close relationship with their child-in-law and believed that their own child had made an unsuitable choice of spouse. Were grandparents simply being wise after the event and allowing their jaundiced feelings about the divorce to colour their judgements? Or do parents generally have reservations about their child's choice of partner whether the decision to marry proves a poor one or not?

Psychoanalysts might point to fathers' unconscious feelings of jealousy to explain the belief that 'nobody is good enough for my little girl' and note that a daughter's choice of partner cuts the 'umbilical cord of authority' (see Rieff, 1959, p 167) and weakens close father–daughter relationships. In his essay, *Totem and taboo*, Freud (1913) drew on material from psychoanalyses and from his knowledge of the customs of primitive tribes to develop ideas about 'father as god' and 'father as king'. These concepts are also discussed in the essays on love (Freud, 1910, 1912, 1918). In the third of these essays Freud commented:

> The husband is almost always so to speak only a substitute, never the right man; it is another man – in typical cases the father – who has the first claim to a woman's love, the husband at most takes second place. (Freud, 1918, p 203)

A more prosaic (although not entirely dissimilar) explanation might call upon a life-course perspective and suggest that emotional feelings surface when significant events reshape personal circumstances and mark transitions in the life course. For some parents, a child's choice of partner or their decision to marry marks a transition point at which the established pattern of family relationships (including close father–daughter relationships) is likely to be disturbed. This may be particularly worrying for parents when their child's relationship appears to contradict their own values that they wanted to propagate in the next generation of their family.

Those grandparents who felt dismayed from the outset about their child's choice of partner usually avoided the possibility of a family rift by maintaining a discreet silence when they were told that the couple intended to marry. A desire to rescue an adult child from a bad decision, however well intentioned, was likely to cause problems in relationships with that child and with his or her choice of partner. Most grandparents resisted the temptation to make their opinions known. Elizabeth's maternal grandparents, however, were dismayed that their daughter had chosen someone who was 18 years older than she, had been divorced before and had children from a previous marriage. They made their views known to their daughter who described the events during her interview.

> There was a blazing row … because I took (partner) over there to meet them and they weren't very happy. They asked me to go over there on my own one day and they told me that they didn't want anything to do with him, that they didn't like him and that they weren't happy with the choice I'd made. For the first six or seven months we were together they had nothing to do with us. I went over there and told them that I was getting married and that they were more than welcome to come to the wedding but if they didn't want to then it would go ahead without them. So they came round and things were better then. (Elizabeth's mother)

Elizabeth's maternal grandmother, now widowed, remembered it as a 'rotten' time in her and her late husband's life. For grandparents in this situation, parental separation may intensify their dislike of their son-in-law and is likely to be perceived as a vindication of their decision to oppose the marriage.

Children or grandchildren?

The comment from Valerie's mother and Ann's maternal grandmother's statement of priorities seemed to suggest that, for some grandparents, grandparenting was a 'satellite' activity: a mere offshoot of the parenting of an adult child. Other cases confirmed the view that parenting rather than grandparenting might have been the grandparents' main priority. Eleanor's mother, who was quoted as saying that she had "had enough" of her ex-husband's parents, went on to describe how she and the paternal grandparents had severed their relationship. This paternal grandmother's desire to take her son's side meant that her ex-daughter-in-law was rejected and, as a consequence, a previously friendly relationship turned sour. What is particularly interesting is that the grandmother's desire to demonstrate solidarity with her son proved more compelling than any desire she might have had to spend time with her grandchild. This not only suggests that her son was more important to her than her granddaughter but was also a further comment on the strong emotions that can accompany grandparents' partisan behaviour. (Grandparents' priorities and the belief that grandparents may be either 'adult-centred' or 'child-centred' in their approach to grandparenting is an issue that was pursued in Chapter Four).

Eleanor's mother believed that the paternal grandmother was not interested in her grandchildren and she seemed to be surprised and disappointed by her ex-mother-in-law's reaction.

> I did ask C's [ex-husband's] mother if she would like to have Eleanor from school one afternoon a fortnight or once a month – have her for tea, pick her up from school. She never got back to me. She doesn't work. She drives a car. I just

> think it's very sad for Eleanor…. I'm sure, they [paternal grandparents] have to take a side. But it's their loss. My children are a wonderful asset to any family and if they don't want them in their family, then it's their loss. I just think it's very sad for all of them. (Eleanor's mother)

Not all grandparents were angry or expressed partisan sentiments. Irene's mother explained that her relationship with one of her husband's friends (whom she had since married) had led to the marital break-up. However, the paternal grandparents not only remained friendly with their ex-daughter-in-law but also made it clear that their grandchildren rather than their adult child remained their main concern.

> Well, there's no argument in our family about it. I never discussed it with [his son] why he divorced. I don't want to know why he divorced, but they are divorced. As I said all along, my thing is for the children. I mean [ex-daughter-in-law] is nice. If she married six or seven times it doesn't affect me at all. The only thing that I'm concerned about is them three children – as long as they get a nice childhood. (Irene's grandfather)

'Not in front of the children'

Maternal grandparents often volunteered the information that they avoided criticising their ex-son-in-law in front of their grandchildren. They felt that they had the right to express their anger to their daughter but that it was important never to allow the children to hear criticisms of their father.

Eleanor's mother complained that her father sometimes forgot the rules and made criticisms of her ex-husband when the children were present. She explained that her father "just can't help himself" and "needs to be picked up on it" whenever he forgets. Eleanor's maternal grandmother also admitted that there was a problem.

> We were so angry and it was difficult for us to be objective because we couldn't slag their father off because they still love their father. That was difficult.

Marion's mother was also concerned that her mother would betray her hostile feelings towards her ex-husband when the children were present. This maternal grandmother, however, felt that she had never broken the 'rules'.

> J [her divorced daughter] sometimes gets a bit uptight when they [the children] mention their father. Say he bought them something for their birthday, I'd say, 'Oh, there's lovely of your father to buy that'. I never run him down to the children. I might run him down to J and G [her husband] but never to the [grand]children. I don't think that's good. (Marion's maternal grandmother)

Janet's maternal grandparents also believed that they had behaved well but rather than praise their son-in-law had adopted the tactic of remaining silent whenever the children talked to them about their father.

> We tried not to put their father in a bad light in their eyes. We tried to avoid doing any of that. Very tempting, but we've deliberately avoided it. So, if the father comes into the conversation, we either remain silent or we say something bland or neutral.... I think we've done it fairly well. (Janet's maternal grandmother)

Grandchildren's views

Children did not talk about their grandparents' partisan behaviour but may simply have been unwilling to talk to the interviewer about such a sensitive subject. They were not, for example, asked directly if their paternal grandparents liked their mother. They did have opportunities to discuss this relationship but some children just provided a curt 'Don't know' when they were asked whether their parents and grandparents had contact. Robert elaborated a little:

> I don't know anything between my dad and nan. Since they [parents] got divorced, I don't know when they seen each other or anything. (Robert, aged 14)

Alfie was aware that his father and his maternal grandparents no longer saw each other, but reassured himself with the thought that there had been no obvious signs of hostility.

> But I haven't heard that they've got a bad relationship, so I suppose that's a good thing. (Alfie, aged 12)

Valerie had learned that her paternal grandparents, who had both died recently, had become embittered by the divorce. It might have been her earlier, happy memories of her grandparents or a feeling that grandparents should be significant people in children's lives that prompted her to add that she regretted that she had not been able to see them.

> When my dad left, they turned against us and they didn't talk to us or anything and they tried to get dad to not like us even more and that was quite horrible. We all used to go as a family, to go and see them with my dad – everyone. And then afterwards we didn't see them since. I wish I did see them before they died. (Valerie, aged 11)

However, we also found that older children were more aware of the tensions.

> *What about the other grandparents? Does your mum go and see them?*

No, I think there's like more tension between them, probably. I think they sort of blame her for the divorce and more. And my dad's sister as well, I think she doesn't like mum particularly. (Alan, aged 16)

Is there a relationship now between your mum and your nan [paternal grandmother]?

No, there isn't. They never talk or anything. If they see each other, they'll just walk the other way but they won't slag each other off or anything. They just think it's best to keep clear.

Did they have a close relationship before?

Yeah, they did, very close really, but not any more. (Belinda, aged 15)

Concluding comments

This chapter has documented the ways in which grandparents explain their partisan feelings and the strength of feelings that they exhibit when they are invited to talk about their ex-children-in-law. Some maternal grandparents appeared to be more hostile towards the ex-spouse than their divorced daughters. Strong emotions were more likely to be generated by a sense of outrage at the way their daughter had been treated than by worries about the negative impact of family break-up on their grandchildren.

When paternal grandparents appeared to be unable to rely on their son to guarantee their future contact with their grandchildren, they were quite likely to befriend their ex-daughter-in-law. They were willing to exchange friendship and practical help for contact with their grandchildren. However, as this chapter has shown, Exchange Theory (see also Chapter Two) does not fully explain the good relationships between grandparents and their ex-sons and daughters-in-law that survived divorce. Many more relationships, we suggest, might have continued on friendly terms had they not seemed unconventional, disloyal or embarrassing. A clean break between paternal grandparents and their ex-daughters-in-law often seemed the 'sensible' course of action although this did not prevent mothers from regretting the loss of friendship with their husband's parents.

The cases in which grandparents strongly disapproved of their adult child's choice of partner led, on occasions, to bitter family quarrels and defiance of parents' wishes. The downside risks of expressing negative views to an adult child who plans to marry are difficult to assess and it is difficult to know whether such quarrels have lasting effects on relationships.

Grandparents who did not take sides or express dislike for their child's ex-spouse appeared to benefit from their refusal to be drawn into the battle. However, these non-partisan grandparents either saw their ex-child-in-law as the guarantee of future contact with their grandchildren or felt strong ties of affection that they were unwilling to abandon. Those who did form friendly relationships, for whatever reason, not only avoided the destructive emotions that characterised some grandparents' thinking but contributed in a positive way to the development of a restructured family that cooperated across the family divide for the benefit of their grandchildren. They did appear to risk some unhappiness for their own divorced child, but this seemed to be a small and probably temporary disadvantage. The reactions of bitterly angry grandparents who had no desire and no motive for renewing contact with their son or daughter-in-law are understandable and a common response to a child's separation and divorce.

Some grandparents suggested that their adult children rather than their grandchildren had remained their main priority. Their grandparenting, described in this chapter as 'a satellite activity', came second to the importance they attributed to their continuing role as a parent.

One widely observed 'rule' of post-divorce grandparenting that emerged from the interviews with parents and grandparents is that children must only hear positive things about their absent father and, in consequence, are usually protected from exposure to their grandparents' bitter feelings. It was impossible to be sure about this because children rarely volunteered information on sensitive subjects; nor were they pressed for answers.

TEN

'Being there': grandparents' financial, emotional and childcare support

Introduction

This chapter examines the range and extent of support that grandparents provided for parents and grandchildren, particularly after a marriage breakdown. We explore parents' assumptions about grandparents' support roles and consider the views of grandparents and their grandchildren about the help that they provided. In particular, we discuss how far grandparents were considered to be under an obligation to provide support, and how they responded to 'a sense of duty'.

Grandparents were usually willing to support their adult children at moments of crisis. Most parents turned to their own parents for help in coping with the immediate effects of separation and divorce. Maternal grandparents were often anxious to do what they could to ameliorate the effects of the divorce. Consequently, they became more involved in childcare and saw their grandchildren more frequently.

Table 3 summarises the results of asking parents how often their children currently saw their grandparents, and how often they saw them when the couple was still married. In most cases, a parent reported their child's contact with grandparents on both sides of the family. In 28 of the 44 families, only the mother was interviewed and in 11 families only the father was interviewed. There were five families in which both parents were interviewed. It was possible

Table 3: Frequency of contact with grandchildren

Annual contact reported by parents	Maternal grandparents before the divorce (38 replies)	Paternal grandparents before the divorce (33 replies)	Maternal grandparents after the divorce (42 replies)	Paternal grandparents after the divorce (37 replies)
Never	0	2 (6%)	2 (5%)	6 (16%)
Between once per annum and once per month	16 (42%)	13 (39%)	15 (36%)	15 (41%)
Between 13 and 52 times per annum	7 (18%)	7 (21%)	5 (12%)	11 (30%)
More than once per week	15 (40%)	11 (33%)	20 (48%)	5 (14%)

in these cases to use the evidence from two parents to confirm the accuracy of the totals provided. Information was obtained from 42 of the 44 families about maternal grandparents' contact but the information about paternal grandparenting was less complete.

The frequencies reported have been converted to annual totals for ease of comparison. Table 3 demonstrates that there was not much difference between the frequency of contact of maternal and paternal grandparents before the divorce. However, as might be expected, there was an increase after the divorce in the numbers of paternal grandparents who rarely or never saw their grandchildren and a decline in the numbers who had very frequent contact. The evidence of this study is that maternal grandparents' childcare duties were likely to increase after their daughter's divorce and those who were in frequent contact before their daughter's separation were likely to intensify their involvement. In contrast, paternal grandparents usually had to depend on their son for contact but some fathers did not have contact, and some of those who did were unwilling to take their children to their grandparents' home.

The link between obligation and affection

Maternal grandparents' involvement with their children and grandchildren could not always be interpreted as evidence of affectionate bonds between the three generations of a divorced family.

Susan's maternal grandmother provided childcare support but was not close to her grandchildren or her daughter. Susan, aged 12, her 13-year-old brother and her 10-year-old sister went to their grandmother's house for a period of two hours or more after school on at least three afternoons each week and for longer periods during the school holidays. This arrangement had enabled their mother to go out to work. Susan's father had allegedly been violent to the children and saw them for a short time every two weeks while their mother was present. Susan's mother described her relationship with her own mother as 'monstrous' and regretted that her divorce had meant that she had had to rely on maternal grandmother's support.

My mother is very, very strict, very regimental and, you know, children are not like that. So it was a very violent relationship ... I can remember how I felt so I don't want the same for my children.... And if I had any other choice, she wouldn't be anywhere near my children, but I have no other choice. A 'wonderful' relationship, isn't it?

Susan did not have paternal grandparents and her maternal grandmother and her father refused to be interviewed. When Susan was interviewed, she explained that she did not like going to her maternal grandmother's house but she recognised it was necessary because it allowed her mother to work. She reported that she tried to behave well but that she "said things in her head" about her grandmother.

> You said you used to say things in your head. What kind of things were they?
>
> Saying 'I hate Nan' and stuff like that. 'I hate Nan 'cos she's telling me off. Can't even have a joke now'.
>
> Susan believed that her grandmother found the arrangement stressful because she is "getting old" and "cannot cope".

This mother's post-divorce arrangements and her dependence on her own mother's support were obviously *not* the result of an affectionate relationship. It would be wrong to see frequency of contact or a willingness to give support as a measure of 'emotional closeness' or to assume that there is always a link between family obligation and affection.

Cherlin and Furstenberg (1985) have suggested that there might, on occasions, be an element of cold calculation in grandparents' deployment of their grandparenting energies. They noted that some grandchildren lived a long way from their grandparents, some had parents that their grandparents did not like and some, as a result of divorce, now had grandchildren who lived with an ex-son or daughter-in-law.

> Under circumstances such as these, grandparents sometimes devote most of their attention to a few grandchildren – or just one. This strategy – which we call 'selective investment' – allows them to act like grandparents and feel satisfied with their role, even although they aren't as close to the rest of their grandchildren. (Cherlin and Furstenberg, 1985, p 97)

Cherlin and Furstenberg argued that grandparents want to enjoy the company of the wider family, talk to their friends about their grandchildren, play with their grandchildren and feel that they are achieving aims that are appropriate to their stage in the life course. They 'play for the long term' and behave in ways that increase the likelihood of securing these benefits. Only diminishing returns of marginal utility would be achieved by extending the strategy to other grandchildren, especially where there are barriers to overcome in the shape of family problems or the grandchildren living a long way from their grandparents' home. A grandchild or grandchildren are therefore 'selected' in order to maximise the return on their grandparents' emotional investment. However, grandparents such as Susan's maternal grandmother, who live near to their divorced adult child, may find it difficult to make such choices. They may feel a strong sense of obligation to help the family even when, as in this case, the request for help comes from a daughter who describes her mother's childcare practices as 'monstrous'.

Supporting the family

After divorce, parents needed to make changes to the previous pattern of family life. They hoped that their children's daily life would be disturbed as little as possible by the divorce and wanted their own parents to support their efforts to restore a sense of normality. Financial support was a key element of the assistance that grandparents might be expected to make. Among the poorest of the families there were examples of grandparents buying food, helping to pay the electricity bills and giving small amounts of money for things that children needed for school.

> I mean, she [paternal grandmother] helps out. For instance, I'm surviving on my £75 a week and I need a roll of wallpaper now and again. I'll ring her up and say, 'Can you pick me up a roll of paper?'. (Karen's father)

Wealthier families provided money to help with the purchase of houses, took the family on holiday and made substantial 'loans' to their adult children. Some dedicated grandparents were involved in picking children up and collecting them daily from school, making their grandchildren's meals and providing substantial amounts of childcare over a number of years while their son or daughter was at work.

Some maternal grandparents appeared to be unselfishly devoted to their daughter and their grandchildren. Others provided temporary help for the divorced family but had other priorities and felt no strong obligation to make a long-term commitment. We wondered what grandparents who gave generous support to their families felt about their role when their adult child separated and divorced.

'Being there' for the children and grandchildren

'Being there' was a phrase that was frequently used to communicate the love and concern that grandparents felt for their children and grandchildren. It seemed to imply a readiness to become involved and to do whatever had to be done to support the family. It was used by grandparents who had made, and perhaps were continuing to make, considerable sacrifices for their divorced children and by those who wanted to say, despite their current lack of involvement, that they would 'be there' if called upon.

> Irene's mother lived near to her parents and her ex-parents-in-law with whom she had a close relationship. She had a new husband, a new baby and three daughters from her previous marriage. Irene (aged 13), her mother and both sets of grandparents were interviewed. The maternal grandfather explained that he felt obliged to 'be there' for his daughter and his grandchildren but that he and his wife were reluctant to become involved in childcare and usually only saw their grandchildren at the local church on Sunday mornings. He believed that his wife was closer to the grandchildren than he was and he explained:

My wife might appear to be more affectionate than I might appear. I don't go out of my way to smother them if you like. But I'm there and they know that I am there if they want. (Irene's maternal grandfather)

Irene's mother expressed surprise and gratitude for the support that her parents showed initially but was immediately critical of the fact that this was not sustained.

But I think if they wanted to see more of their grandchildren, they would make the effort. I don't really think they make much of an effort. My mum will occasionally ring up.... They only see them in church on a Sunday morning. They might see them for ten minutes. They don't visit them really. (Irene's mother)

Irene's grandfather, who saw 'being there' as a kind of 'stand by' or 'on call' duty, was quite open about his reluctance to become involved with his grandchildren who lived only a couple of miles away.

I tend to disappear. Well, they all want to do different things and for some of them the attention span isn't good.... One jumps on, the other jumps off. They are all shouting. You can see that one will be winding up the other to see what they will do. (Irene's maternal grandfather)

The message from divorced parents confirmed the view that grandparents are expected to 'be there' for their families. Many divorced mothers believed that their parents had an *obligation* to give generous support both to help them to cope with childcare after divorce and to support their children. However, it is clear that a small minority of grandparents is unwilling to become involved and reluctant to provide support for their divorced families. Further, not all grandparents wanted to make sacrifices for their grandchildren, although this was not always easy for them to admit. One reluctant set of maternal grandparents who saw little of their grandchildren explained that they were available if needed but did not want to appear 'too possessive'.

Kate's mother provided a clear account of her expectations of her parents.

Kate's mother lived with her parents during the first few months of her separation but now had a home of her own. From the outset, she seemed to assume that the maternal grandparents had an obligation to fill a gap in their grandchildren's lives that had been created by her divorce. Initially, the grandparents had not wanted to become involved because they felt their daughter should take charge of her own affairs but Kate's mother interpreted their desire not to interfere as 'holding back' and this was not, in her view, compatible with good grandparenting. Her assumption was that her parents' reluctance could only be explained by their uncertainty about their grandparenting role. She felt that she needed to reassure them that it was appropriate to become involved. She did not consider the possibility that they might have had their own reasons for wanting to maintain some distance between themselves and their divorced family.

> My son should be closer [to his maternal grandparents].... I say to him [grandfather], 'You take him to rugby and you be the man in his life. It's okay'. But my father gets confused about that. H [Kate's younger brother] doesn't really have a male role model except my father. I think our family tend to hold back and think that it's her [mother's] life, we don't want to get in the way and cross the boundaries. It's my business. They did that with my son and I know that they have upset my sister-in-law because she says, 'Well why don't you come and see our little boy?'. My mother would say, 'I don't like to go down there. I wait to be invited', and things like this. (Kate's mother)

Although she realised that supporting her and her children would be a burden to her parents, she was disappointed that help was not immediately volunteered:

> I said, 'You are going to have to look after me and the children and the cat and the furniture until the housing association give me somewhere to live'.

Help was often needed until parents had had sufficient time to solve the problems associated with reorganising family life. However, for some mothers, the grandparents became the solution in the sense that the pattern of family life established after divorce depended crucially on maternal grandparents' long-term commitment to their divorced child and their grandchildren. In the years after their divorce, these mothers came to depend on this high level of support to sustain their version of post-divorce parenting.

'Being there' for the grandchildren was such a potent social obligation that it was difficult to avoid its consequences. Despite this, our equally powerful taboos about interference with parenting and a general acceptance of parents' rights to bring up their children as they see fit have created an imbalance in the socially imposed expectations on grandparents. Eleanor's mother had received lots of financial and practical support from her parents after her divorce. She described how generous her parents had been. The maternal grandparents had taken Eleanor and her mother on holiday to the US. During the holiday, however, Eleanor's grandfather had reprimanded Eleanor, and the mother had objected strongly to her father's intervention.

> They paid for our holidays, they took us away on holiday and they would take the children out for outings, and mum would buy them vests and pants and all the things that you don't want to have to buy because you can't see them – she'd do that.... We were in America on holiday. Eleanor wanted ketchup on her breakfast and my dad said, 'You've already had enough'.... So we came to blows over it and it was really pathetic [sighs]. But I said, 'She's my daughter and if she wants ketchup and I say she can, she can and she will'. (Eleanor's mother)

It is easy in our culture to be persuaded that grandparents have a duty to become involved when their adult child and their grandchildren encounter a family crisis. But it is just as credible to assert that they ought not to interfere with matters that are the responsibility of the parents. It is a situation that makes grandparents open to exploitation and vulnerable to criticism.

The 'grandparent as parent' continuum

The roles of grandparent and parent are usually distinct. The responsibility for children's upbringing primarily lies with the parents (hence the importance for parents and grandparents of the norm of non-interference). Grandparents' relationship with their grandchildren may include some responsibility for childcare but most grandparents would not consider their occasional contributions to their grandchildren's physical care, socialisation and education to be a defining characteristic of their role. For many grandparents, enjoying their grandchildren's company and being interested in their growth and development is seen as central. Parenting is an aspect of grandparenting but not necessarily a defining feature.

However, the extent to which grandparents had adopted the role of substitute parents after divorce proved to be a useful dimension on which to classify their approach to grandparenting. Grandparents who were providing substantial amounts of childcare were at one end of the continuum; at the other extreme, there were grandparents who were distant emotionally, geographically or both. At the mid-point of the continuum, were grandparents who were able to concentrate on enjoying their grandchildren's company without assuming major childcare responsibilities. For many grandparents and grandchildren, this mid-point seemed to represent the ideal circumstances in which the grandparent–grandchild relationship could flourish. We wondered, therefore, what grandparents who acted as substitute parents to their grandchildren thought about their situation. What did they feel about the commitment that they had made? Their adult child's divorce provided an opportunity to become more involved. Did their involvement add a whole new dimension to life that they might have missed if their adult child had not divorced? Did they ever feel resentment at having to support their families in such a significant way?

The grandparents' views

We look first at three families in which the maternal grandparents provided essential childcare for their grandchildren on at least five occasions each week. Janet, Jane and Marion had grandparents who had a major commitment to childcare and need to be distinguished from those who saw a lot of their grandchildren for 'non-essential' reasons (for example, grandchildren who call at their grandparents' house on the way home from school). Did they enjoy the experience of playing a major part in caring for their grandchildren?

Janet's maternal grandparents collected Janet (aged 9) and her younger brother from school every day at half past three and looked after them until 6 o'clock when their mother returned from work. She would stay at her parents' house for a short time and then take the children home. Janet's mother was asked whether her parents' relationship with the children had changed since her separation.

I think they are not grandparents anymore. My dad is more of a disciplinarian with them now than perhaps he should be. I think, perhaps, it has taken away the fun of just being a grandparent.

Why do you think he thinks that?

Oh, no, I am not saying he does. But they [the children] haven't got a male influence and my son especially needs a male influence.

So you are pleased about it?

Well, yes in a way, but in a way no, because my dad has already been through that role hasn't he? He's already done the fathering bit. He doesn't need to do it again with my son, so I think perhaps it's taken the shine off just messing around with them. They've got a bit more responsibility for them.

Have you talked to him about this?

No. No. He just said – it was just a casual comment one day – he said, 'Oh, it's not fun anymore'.

Janet's grandfather revealed that this was not just a passing comment but a major issue.

What I feel is we are not being given the opportunity to be grandparents. We're surrogate parents in a way. That's my bug.

That's an interesting comment.

We see them everyday. We have work to do. We have to get on with things and invariably we see them around teatime. We feed them. We water them and we do the things that have to be done for them and therefore it is work – we're working. You're not spending time playing, enjoying their company. And they're not enjoying our company in the way that I envisaged my grandchildren would. They get on with their things and we're doing our things and we mix in with them from time to time, but it isn't – what's that term they use these days? It isn't 'quality time'. (Janet's maternal grandfather)

Janet's mother had been given a brief glimpse of her father's feeling that her divorce had deprived him of a 'proper' grandparenting role but the depth of his disappointment had not been discussed openly. Janet's grandmother revealed that her close involvement with her grandchildren was not new. She had supported her other daughter (in an intact family) and had helped to care for her grandchild while her parents were at work.

> And of course we don't see her [grandchild in intact family] as much as the other two [in the divorced family]. We used to, because we used to pick her up from nursery – and school when she started. Well, we picked her up from nursery first of all. We had her two afternoons then and then when she went to school. They only did half days, so we used to go up to B [30 miles away] twice a week to pick her up and then we used to have her in the afternoon. (Janet's maternal grandmother talking about the support she had provided for her other daughter's child)

These grandparents' devoted service to their family could be depended on for the foreseeable future. Their sacrifice was not just a response to a temporary crisis but an intensification of an approach to grandparenting that they had practised before their daughter's separation.

> Jane's maternal grandparents looked after their grandchildren on five days each week. Their daughter had come to depend on them when she came to live near her parents while she was still married. She had since divorced and was now remarried but the high level of support had continued after her remarriage. Their granddaughter was dropped at their house at 7.50am, and after school the child remained at her grandparents' house until her mother and stepfather returned from work. When Jane's parents were still married these grandparents had given an extraordinary amount of help.

> I used to have to take her to playgroup in the morning. She didn't go every morning. She only went three times a week and then of course she went to nursery half day and then full-time school. So I have had her since she was two-and-a-half, really. We still have her now but only for that three quarters of an hour in the morning and then I have her here from half past three until about quarter past to half past five. (Jane's maternal grandmother)

When the couple separated, however, it became clear that their daughter and granddaughter were going to need more support than had been anticipated. The grandparents gave their daughter substantial financial help, lots of emotional support and provided more childcare for their grandchild. More than four years after the divorce the support continued. These grandparents had been supportive when Jane's parents were married, had graduated to temporary substitute parent when they separated and, since the divorce, had become the long-term solution to their daughter's post-divorce parenting problems. There was, it seemed, little reason for Jane's mother to seek out other childcare arrangements even after her remarriage but Jane's maternal grandparents were not happy about the impact that their daughter's divorce had had on their lives. On the day of the interview, Jane, her mother and her stepfather were on holiday and the grandparents had a free day. They explained that they had gone out to lunch and had enjoyed the unaccustomed luxury of not having to watch the clock to ensure they were back in time to meet their grandchild from school. They confessed that they had been adopting a strategy of taking short breaks to escape their grandparental duties.

Grandmother: People say, 'Off on holiday again?', and I say, 'Yes because when we are at home our time is not our own'. If I go to town I have got to rush back. We have only got another 12 months. And I think then, when she goes to the other [secondary] school, she [granddaughter] will not want us so much then.

Grandfather: She definitely won't want us then.

Marion's maternal grandparents were well aware that their support for their two granddaughters had become essential.

As God is willing and I hope we survive until we're older. All we've prayed for is we can see those children get into their teens because at the moment the little one is too young to be left. But it's the little one we couldn't leave and if God is willing I hope we can cope, as I don't know how they would manage. (Marion's maternal grandmother)

The maternal grandparents provided childcare on two nights each week when the mother was on night-duty and every day during the school holidays. In addition, they went to the house in time to meet their grandchildren from school, make their evening meal and stay with them until their daughter returned from work. Marion's mother received no financial support from her ex-husband, did not have a new partner and never went out in the evenings except to work. Her parents recognised the hardships that she was suffering and were devoted to her and their grandchildren. However, like other grandparents, they had ambivalent feelings and some regrets. The strain of having to act as parents to children whose father, as they saw it, had deserted their daughter, made them angry but the thought that they might reduce the amount of help that their daughter depended on was never considered.

Grandmother: Well there is nothing to change. There is nothing we can do. I wish I could go off for the day to town. I see my neighbours all retired going off with their husbands. We could not do it…. When he [maternal grandfather] retired, we thought we would have a nice little life and go off somewhere. But we cannot. I'm not grumbling, but I am in a way.

The grandfather, an ex-railway employee, had a pass that allowed him to travel free on the trains: "I can travel all over the country for nothing, but we can't go".

Marion's mother explained that her parents had been involved in helping to bring up her children almost since the birth of her first child because her husband refused to look after the children while she was on night-duty.

So they [maternal grandparents] have always been involved somewhere along the line with their care – their day-to-day care. Since we've split up, obviously, they have to do a lot more. (Marion's mother)

These cases involved older, retired, maternal grandparents who had become substitute parents to their grandchildren. In all three families, the maternal grandparents had not suddenly been recruited to help their daughters when their marriages ended. There had been a history of considerable involvement before the marriage break-up. Despite their willingness to help, they were aware that their life had been restricted and the anticipated joys of retirement had been curtailed. Some complained about ex-sons-in-law who were, in their view, making no financial provision or inadequate financial provision for the children. Most, however, did not mention the legal system and did not have suggestions for how public policy might support them or relieve their burden. For the families in this study, supporting adult children and grandchildren after a family break-up was discussed as 'a family matter' and not something in which there should be legal or state involvement.

Parents' perceptions of grandparents' support

We asked how parents felt about the contribution that grandparents were making. Were they aware of the reservations that their parents felt about their involvement in childcare?

Marion's mother was effusive in her praise and full of admiration for the way in which her parents had supported her and their grandchildren.

Brilliant! Absolutely brilliant! They are like second parents actually. My father, I think they consider my father more their father than their own. They don't like to think that he's my father. He belongs to them. They have got an absolutely brilliant relationship with him.

Jane's mother was matter of fact and was either unaware of her parents' feelings or chose not to mention that she knew that her dependence on them for childcare was inhibiting their own plans for retirement. Although she had remarried, she felt that she had no choice but to continue to rely on her parents.

I knew when I got divorced I would be highly reliant on them for baby-sitting. In the morning I drop her off there about quarter to eight. She walks to school now herself at half eight and she walks home herself and I usually pick her up anytime between

> half four and quarter past five. They [maternal grandparents] do things like take her to gymnastics for me.

There had, however, been a hint of the tension that was revealed in the grandparents' interview. However, Jane's mother's reaction to the emergence of conflict was to say nothing for fear of disturbing the arrangements that she had come to rely on.

> [Jane] says nanny fusses too much, but she realises that she hasn't got a choice. If she wants to do things and have things, then I have to work. She has got a bit of a temper, she's very self-determined, so am I, so is my mother, so there's three characters who can easily rub each other up the wrong way. I know that it's better sometimes not to say anything because I'll only regret it and I know I am dependent upon them for looking after her.

Like Janet's mother, who sensed her father's disappointment but chose not to pursue the matter, Jane's mother also decided that it was sensible to ignore the evidence that the burden of childcare was causing her parents problems. Despite her obvious dependency on her parents, she saw herself as 'self-reliant' and gave no hint of a feeling that the level of support given by her parents was unusual.

> I do tend to be very self-reliant. I tend to cope quite well.

In contrast, Marion's mother was well aware of the sacrifices that her parents were making.

> *Was it a strain on them?*
>
> Not on a financial side but probably on an emotional side. I was having to rely on them a lot more for childcare for me to go out to work. It meant every weekend. They've had no weekends to themselves for the last five years. I've worked every weekend. Their life has actually more or less been put on hold. (Marion's mother)

Grandchildren's reactions

As noted earlier, some mothers appeared not to recognise, or did not want to recognise, that their own parents were making sacrifices, and some grandchildren's reactions were much the same. The children's comments seemed to be 'second hand', in the sense that they reflected what their mothers had told them. Others did not appear to realise that their relationship with their maternal grandparents involved childcare and support for the family. Their grandparents were often taken for granted. Children were unaware, and probably did not need to know, that they and their divorced parent had to depend on their grandparents. 'Putting life on hold', sacrificing the freedom of retirement and acting as a substitute parent for grandchildren might have earned some mothers' gratitude and admiration but it did not necessarily impress the grandchildren for whom the sacrifices were being made. Marion was quite critical of her 'lazy' grandmother who devoted a good deal of her life to looking after her two grandchildren.

> My nan is all lazy and she talks a lot and stuff and she always wants to sit down because she's got a bad back.

> *Does your sister like these grandparents?*

> I'm not too sure about my nan but I know that she likes grampy to come. She [my nan] always tells her off and she's chatty and lazy.

Jane (aged 9) had also not recognised that her grandparents were making major sacrifices to support her:

> *Are your grandparents helpful to you or your mum in any way you can think of?*

> Yes, sometimes. Like if we go on holiday, when we come back, they look after our cat.

When Norman (aged 10) was asked the same question, he was aware of the help that his maternal grandparents had given to him and his mother. His answer also revealed a little of the memories that children may retain of a family break-up which for Norman was when he was around seven years of age. He was still close to his maternal grandparents who had been a reassuringly 'fixed point' at a moment when his life must have seemed insecure.

> *Do your mum's parents help your mum in any way?*

> They did a little bit, they calmed her down when she started to cry and they put their arms around each other.

> *Did they help you?*

> They cared for me and looked after me through all the stuff [family break-up].

Paternal grandparents who are there for 'the other side'

A few paternal grandparents gave practical help and moral support to their ex-daughters-in-law. It was not simply that they did not display any of the partisan feelings that were discussed in Chapter Five: they had chosen to 'be there' for the 'other side' of the divorced family. In accordance with Exchange Theory (see Chapter Two), were these grandparents exchanging their friendship and support for opportunities to maximise contact with their grandchildren? Were this true, we would expect that these grandparents would not have been able to see their grandchildren as often without their ex-daughter-in-law's support. We were able to explore this possibility with some of the grandparents.

Jane's maternal grandparents (see page 111) were substantially involved in providing childcare support for Jane's mother. However, Jane's *paternal* grandparents had also given Jane's mother and her new husband a considerable amount of support. They had quarrelled with their son over his adultery (that had led to the break-up of the family). He and his new wife had severed their relationship with them. They had visited their ex-daughter-in-law frequently since the separation. The paternal grandfather had also stayed for several weeks to complete some building work on his ex-daughter-in-law's new house.

Ann's mother also had a close relationship with her ex-parents-in-law. When she was asked why the friendship had developed after the divorce she recalled that it was her parents-in-law who had taken the initiative because they feared they would lose contact with their grandchildren. Ann's paternal grandmother confirmed this view and demonstrated the depth of emotion that the fear of losing contact with her grandchildren had created. Even the effort of remembering how she felt caused her to bust into tears during the interview.

Did you have a good relationship with your daughter-in-law during the marriage?

Yes, but I'd like to think that we've got a stronger one now. I didn't want to lose the children [starts crying] – that was my biggest fear, that I wouldn't see them.

Charles' paternal grandparents were close to him and they had been generous and helpful to their ex-daughter-in-law. Charles (aged 13) explained that after the divorce, his mother had been surprised to discover that his paternal grandparents still cared about her:

The people we went to was my mum's parents because it was like they were my mum's side and mum didn't think that S and M [the paternal grandparents] would, like, really matter. But they *did* care about mum.

Charles' mother reported that her ex-husband never saw his son and had not made any efforts to remain in contact with him.

Diana's mother had maintained a relationship with her ex-mother-in-law but it was not a close one and she expressed reservations. Her ex-husband had severed relationships with his mother and had refused, against his new wife's wishes, to invite her to the wedding when he had remarried. In a recent telephone call, Diana's paternal grandmother had said, "I know he's remarried but you will always be my daughter-in-law".

None of these paternal grandparents, who had remained friendly with their ex-daughters-in-law, could have kept in contact with their grandchildren without the support of the resident parent. Friendship and support did appear to have been exchanged for contact with grandchildren. Jane's maternal grandmother explained the thinking succinctly:

> Well if they [paternal grandparents] don't keep in touch [with mother] they lose all contact with Jane. That's the thing with grandparents, it doesn't matter who is at fault: they want to keep in touch.

Paternal grandparents who maintained contact with their grandchildren through their father did not usually provide support for an ex-daughter-in-law. However, Irene's family (discussed earlier in this chapter) was an exception and did not confirm the hypothesis that grandparents' desire to secure contact with their grandchildren explained why they continued to provide support for their child's ex-spouse. Irene's father had agreed lower maintenance payments with his ex-wife in exchange for looking after his three children at weekends. Irene's mother explained that two of the three children had stormy relationships with their father. He worked most weekends that the children were with him and went out in the evenings when he got back from work. There had been family rows about his alleged lack of care but his parents had enjoyed lots of contact with their grandchildren and had maintained a close relationship with their ex-daughter-in-law. If this father was indeed as unreliable as his ex-wife alleged and did not get on well with two of his three daughters, it is possible that his parents were offering support in order to secure contact with their grandchildren for the future. The case, however, was the only one that was not entirely consistent with the hypothesis that the need for contact with grandchildren provided a motive for paternal grandparents' support for an ex-daughter-in-law.

Maternal grandparents and their ex-sons-in-law

Other examples of grandparents' good relationships with both sides of the divorced family included two families in which the parents shared care of their children (see the discussion of Ingrid's and Debbie's families in Chapter Six of this book). Affectionate relationships between maternal grandparents and their daughter's ex-husband were comparatively rare because, in most cases, the mother was the resident parent and maternal grandparents' contact with their grandchildren was secure. Shared care arrangements, we surmise, can bring maternal grandparents closer to an ex-son-in-law because he has a part to play in caring for their grandchildren. However, it was not possible to test this idea because there were only two sets of divorced parents who shared care of their children and in the case of Ingrid's parents there had been a highly amicable divorce. Carl's father had initially assumed full-time responsibility for his children and the close relationship that he had developed with his parents-in-law continued after the divorce. His ex-wife explained that her parents had been a great source of support for her ex-husband.

> When this divorce happened, if my mum and dad hadn't been there, I don't know what would have happened to [ex-husband]. My mum and dad were a tower of strength for him. They were there all the way for him. They'd help him in every way they could; they were there as a mum and dad. (Carl's mother)

George's family was another that did not fit the profile. The maternal grandparents had a close relationship with George's father even though the mother was the resident parent. As in the case of Ingrid's parents, this had also been a very amicable divorce. George's mother commented, "We're an odd couple. We get on well", and added:

> They [maternal grandparents] made it very clear to him [George's father] that he was as welcome as he'd ever been. They made an effort to make sure he knew he was still involved in family things. People do think we're a bit strange. Both of us wanted the best for the children.

Given the rarity of these close relationships in our study, we suspect that relatively few divorced couples and their ex-parents-in-law remain on such friendly terms after their divorce.

Concluding comments

Maternal grandparents' contact with grandchildren may increase after parental divorce should they become increasingly involved in caring for their grandchildren. In contrast, those paternal grandparents who have to depend on their sons for contact may discover that their opportunities to see their grandchildren have diminished. Grandparents felt a strong sense of family obligation that was reinforced by parents' expectations that they would offer financial, emotional and childcare support. Meeting parents' expectations could become excessively burdensome and not all grandparents were willing to provide substantial amounts of childcare. In Chapter Three, it was suggested that a 'reluctant–enthusiastic' continuum might be a helpful way of classifying grandparents' behaviour, and the evidence presented in this chapter confirmed this. We also discussed a 'grandparent-as-parent–grandparent-as-grandparent' continuum that drew attention to the differences that responsibility for childcare can make to the grandparent–grandchild relationship. 'Being there' for the grandchildren is something that may bring its own rewards, enhance grandparents' lives and provide them with the satisfaction of knowing that they have fulfilled their obligations to their family. However, grandparents who lived near their daughter could find themselves much more committed to the divorced family than they had intended.

Those grandparents who felt that their childcare duties had become burdensome and stressful might have felt guilty about harbouring such feelings. They were not willing to discuss them openly with their divorced child and, in their interviews, presented the issue as a family matter with few, if any, public policy implications. Parents and grandchildren were often unaware of the difficulties grandparents encountered. Nevertheless, there is evidence that some grandparents harbour reservations and would benefit from measures that would relieve them from the strain that they undoubtedly feel. Friendly relationships between fathers and maternal grandparents, in this study, were rare; those that existed between paternal grandparents and resident mothers may have been developed in order to allow these paternal grandparents to secure contact with grandchildren.

ELEVEN

Excluded grandparents

Introduction

This chapter discusses the minority of cases in our study in which the grandchild–grandparent relationship was seriously disrupted after parental divorce. Such cases can be seen as lying at the extreme end of our third continuum of grandparenting styles – the 'grandparent as partisan supporter' continuum, discussed in Chapter Nine of this book. By this, we mean the extent to which grandparents took sides after the break-up, and assumed attitudes and behaviour reflecting what they saw as the 'rights and wrongs' of their divorced child's situation. In some cases, grandchildren had been used as pawns in the conflict between the two sides of the divided family. We ask why some grandparents in our study were deprived of contact with their grandchildren and why some parents thought their children's relationships with their grandparents should not survive the break-up.

This chapter also draws on interviews with members of the Grandparents' Association, the leading support and pressure group for grandparents. We turn first to the grandparents in the Cardiff study who could be described as 'excluded'. Why had they encountered difficulties in remaining in touch with their grandchildren?

The families

Bitter divorces

It has long been argued that parents of divorced sons can become the victims of the fall-out from their ex-daughter-in-law's anger. Kruk and Hall (1995) and Drew and Smith (1999) found that maternal grandparents' relationships with grandchildren were generally unaffected by divorce, but noted that paternal grandparents need to 'tread cautiously'. Drew and Smith (1999, p 194) commented:

> If the grandchild resides with the mother who moves away from the father, or if there is unresolved conflict between the former spouses, then access may be withheld from the father, and thereby from the paternal grandparents.

In six of the 44 families in our study, a mother had prevented her ex-husband from contacting the children after the couple had separated and divorced. In five of these cases, there was at least one paternal grandparent alive who was no longer able to maintain contact with his or her grandchild. Perhaps the most difficult of these cases was that of Annabel's father and paternal grandmother who had been denied contact with Annabel.

Annabel's parents had been divorced for four years and the father's contact with his daughter had been sporadic during this period. It had, at the time of the interview, been more than a year since he had been allowed contact of any kind with Annabel (aged 8).

In his interview, Annabel's father made it clear that regaining contact with Annabel was important to him and to his mother, who had seen her granddaughter almost every day before he and his wife had separated more than five years earlier. He showed the researcher a child's bedroom full of Christmas and birthday presents that awaited his daughter's return and produced copies of letters vehemently denying the accusations that his wife had made. He claimed that Annabel was afraid to comment on her mother's accusations because his ex-wife and her new husband would have punished her had she dared to take her father's side in this increasingly bitter dispute.

I went back to court twice with court orders because every time the holidays were coming my ex-wife would make some excuse so that my daughter wouldn't come – always trying to cause problems. I would go to court, I would get Annabel back and everything would be perfect. Then my ex-wife was doing things in the background, running to social services saying things. (Annabel's father)

Annabel's father blamed the courts for failing to support him more effectively.

It's the men who are treated badly by the courts and social services. You never see the same judge twice and you see them looking through their notes just before you start. They don't really care. I would like to see the government doing more to get us equal treatment and greater fairness. (Annabel's father)

Annabel's paternal grandmother commented:

For the first few years I couldn't sleep and I would write out my thoughts. One time I wrote a letter, thinking it would be helpful at court [although it didn't get there]. I sort of drafted things out. (Annabel's paternal grandmother)

The letter was an account of this grandmother's relationship with her grandchild. It began:

I would see her almost daily as I live only yards away from the flat where she was born and brought up. I was often invited for Sunday dinner, and when Annabel was old enough she loved me to go to her bedroom with her to play.

The final paragraph of her letter said:

> So you can see that Annabel and I had a very close relationship. Annabel was a child who loved the life she led and loved her parents and has always had a close relationship with her dad who adores her.

Annabel's grandmother also alleged that Annabel's mother and her new husband were attempting to persuade Annabel to tell her father that she did not want to see him again. She recalled an incident that had happened over a year ago:

> My son then asked Annabel what was the matter at the time and she said that they [mother and her new partner] had both shook her and shook her before she came down to try to make her tell her father that she didn't want to be with him. (Annabel's paternal grandmother)

It is impossible for a research team to know whether or not the mother's refusal to allow her ex-husband to see her child was simply an act of vindictiveness or whether her ex-husband, as she alleged, had been guilty of maltreating his daughter. Kaganas and Piper (2001) have taken up the question of how the judicial system should react to a parent's unlawful refusal to comply with its decisions (see also Advisory Board on Family Law: Children Act Sub-Committee, 2002). They note that to embark on a course of action that might ultimately lead to a mother being imprisoned would not be in the family's best interests, and that courts do not allow "parental authority easily to be undermined by third parties" (see p 267). The welfare of children, they add, is a 'good' that all can agree on and in family conflicts "the unity and autonomy of the nuclear family may be seen as most important for children's welfare" (Kaganas and Piper, 2001, p 268). The Director of the Grandparents' Association agreed that for some grandparents a successful court action did not mean that they could see their grandchildren:

> There are a few [grandparents] who do take legal action. They often write to us and say that they have won. They are on a high. But then the sad part comes. An awful lot of them get back to us to say that they are disappointed because the parents are breaking the court order. Judges will not send mothers of young children to jail for contempt of court. What was a high point has become a hollow victory.

She believed that there was an increasing tendency for members of the Grandparents' Association, who tried to win court orders to restore contact with their grandchildren, to be accused of child abuse by the parents who opposed them. In Annabel's case, there was no suggestion that her paternal grandmother had been guilty of any abuse but her contact with her grandchild had ended because of a dispute between her son and her ex-daughter-in-law.

Had the paternal grandmother taken court action and won the right to spend time with her granddaughter, she would almost certainly have arranged for Annabel to spend time with her father. Annabel's mother refused to be interviewed but she may well have argued that it was fear of the father's continuing maltreatment of Annabel rather than any outcome of divorce that had led to the paternal grandmother losing all contact with her grandchild.

Resignation and defeat

Not all parents and grandparents who wanted contact with children were as determined as Annabel's father and her paternal grandmother.

> Karen's maternal grandparents, who lived in another part of the country, were 'reluctant grandparents'. Karen's father, who had been treated for depression, had decided to drop his bid for contact with his children because "there was too much stress involved". He did not feel that his mother would be upset at the loss of contact with her grandchildren, and his ex-wife reported:
>
> > I never really hit it off with his mother at all, not since I had my second son, and I have no contact with her and I have absolutely no wish to. He [ex-husband] did put in an application and I was contacted by the Court Welfare Officer. But he [ex-husband] dropped his application because he was married before and he said that he didn't want to go through the same process again. And I can understand that because it would probably put him back into hospital. I am quite happy with that actually, because I don't want him to have contact with the children. I stopped contact because I can't justify putting my children into the hands of someone who has mental health problems.
>
> In her interview, however, Karen (aged 9) expressed her sadness at not seeing her father or her paternal grandmother. Her continuing loyalty to both sides of her divorced family was characteristic of many children in this study (see Chapter Eight of this book).
>
> > I saw her [paternal grandmother] at Christmas 2000. That was the last time.
>
> *What happened?*
>
> > We had lots of nuts and Smarties and my nan and me were playing with my pony and the Barbie that she got me.... She let us see the fish in the fish pond and let us feed them and we used to plant some plants.
>
> *There is a pond in the garden?*
>
> > Yes and she used to let me touch the fish. I haven't seen my dad since this Christmas [14 months ago].

Her father, who was interviewed a few weeks later, confirmed his ex-wife's version of events and admitted that he had simply abandoned hope.

> I don't see them. No, not at present. It's ongoing in the courts at the moment, but I – I mean, having been there once before – it's my second divorce. I'm really not prepared to go through all that again. Because I had it all in the first marriage and if they [mothers] don't want you to see the kids, it's like the divorce isn't it – you just have to let it happen.

Karen's father's resignation, in the face of what he believed to be overwhelming odds, meant that the paternal grandmother would not be able to renew her relationship with her grandchildren.

Steve's father had been divorced twice and the paternal grandparents discovered that they were not allowed to see their grandchildren from either of their son's marriages. They felt powerlessness when faced with their daughter-in-law's refusal to let them see their grandchildren from her son's second marriage.

What do you think about not seeing them?

> Well it's upsetting really, but I have cried so much over them [the grandchildren from their son's first marriage] that I can't go through with it. But if it is going to cause hassle then I would rather not bother and I know her mother [maternal grandmother] don't like us anyway. So rather than make a fuss and go to court I would rather just leave it.... It just hurts when people say how many grandchildren have you got and I say I don't really see them and, you know, they just look. (Steve's paternal grandmother)

In both Steve's and Karen's families, the acrimonious relationships that existed between the paternal grandmothers and their ex-daughters-in-law had developed some years before the separation took place.

Successful outcomes

Oliver's paternal grandmother did not did not get on well with her ex-daughter-in-law who had a daughter from a previous marriage. She complained that Oliver's mother had wanted to "push her out" and rely entirely on her own family. As a result she had not been able to play the grandmother role with Oliver (aged 10) and his younger brother in the way that she had hoped during the years that her son had been married.

When the couple separated, Oliver's paternal grandmother found that she was no longer able to see her grandsons and claimed that her daughter-in-law's first husband and his family had been treated in the same way.

> We told her that we would go through the courts to fight.... I went to see my own solicitor and said that if she continued to try to stop me from seeing them I would have to go to court. When she [Oliver's mother] found out about it she backed off and changed her mind.

In this case, the hostilities had begun long before the break-up but the threat of legal proceedings was sufficient to cause Oliver's mother to reconsider.

> Pauline's mother, who had now remarried, had prevented her ex-husband from seeing Pauline and her brother and sister for a period of several months. Pauline's father was asked whether his parents had thought about going to court when they discovered that they could not have contact with their grandchildren.

> They wanted to get involved because they weren't allowed to see them as well and they wanted to see the kids. It's grandparents' rights. But 'the social' [social services] said that if they went and reported them [mother and her new husband] of cruelty to the children of not seeing their grandparents then there might have been a case. But then she [ex-wife] accused my parents of treating the kids bad.

> When Pauline's father was asked whether his parents had seen a solicitor, he revealed that they had made an initial enquiry but had discovered that they could not afford to take the matter further.

> So I said that there was no need for them to spend the money because I said that when I have them you'll see them. So they were happy then. And that has worked out brilliant. My mother has a big house and a big garden and they can go out to play and my mother is happy to see them, and my mother does their tea. My father works on Saturday but he comes home in his dinner hour to see them.

> The paternal grandfather explained that when he had been to see a solicitor he had been given a copy of "the rules" – a written explanation of the procedure – and had been told that it would cost about £2,000. This was a lot more than he could afford.

Fathers who severed contact with their own parents

Divorced fathers generally had good relationships with their own parents and wanted to take their children to their home where there might be more space to play and where children would be cared for and entertained. In four cases, however, the paternal grandparents had become excluded, not because their ex-daughter-in-law was bitterly angry but because they had quarrelled with their divorced son who might otherwise have brought their grandchildren to see them. Jane's family has been chosen to illustrate the point.

Jane's paternal grandparents had a close relationship with Jane's mother and were an example of paternal grandparents who were able to maintain contact with their grandchild because they offered friendship and support to their ex-daughter-in-law. When they were interviewed, however, these paternal grandparents wanted to talk about their son [Jane's father] and his new family. Jane's father had remarried about three years ago and he and his new wife now had two infant children.

Jane's paternal grandmother explained that she had been outraged when she was told that her son was having an affair with a colleague at work. She told him that she disapproved of his conduct and her son's new partner reacted strongly to her intervention. The affair led to the divorce and when Jane's father remarried, he and his new wife would not allow his parents any form of contact with their new grandchildren. Jane's paternal grandparents described the day they had gone to the town where their son lived only to discover that his wife and their grandchildren were not there.

> We did send them Christmas presents but they were returned and a nasty letter accompanied them.

> We've been down to [town X]. We phoned before we went to say, 'Can we see the grandchildren?'. When we got there our son was on his own so we said, 'Where are the grandchildren?'. He said, 'They're in [town Y] but she's on her way back'.... When it came to four o'clock, she still hadn't arrived. She was in hiding. She just didn't want to see us and didn't want us to see the grandchildren. So we came back without seeing them and we were told not to go again. (Jane's paternal grandmother)

Although Jane's paternal grandmother had initially wanted to talk about the outcome of her son's divorce, she found during the interview that the subject too painful. In her interview, Jane's mother explained that she had tried to intervene by writing to her ex-husband to ask him to allow his parents to see their new grandchildren but her letter had had no effect.

> I feel that they [ex-husband and his new wife] are just storing up trouble for the future by not letting [the children] know they've got another set of grandparents. I said, 'You are denying them a basic human right to see their grandparents'. They'll only ask in the future where are their daddy's parents. Why haven't you let me see them? (Jane's mother)

It should be noted that these accounts of excluded grandparents' attempts to restore contact with their grandchildren are one-sided. In most cases, one side of the family was keen to talk to a researcher and describe the emotional turmoil that they had suffered after divorce while the other side was not. Mothers who had tried to prevent their ex-husbands from seeing the children, and fathers who had ended their relationship with their own parents, were unwilling to be interviewed. Requests were met with a refusal or, more often, with no response at all. Grandparents considered that parents were simply being vindictive and felt that they and their grandchildren had been deprived of the benefits of an important relationship.

Such cases prompt the question, 'Why should grandparents in divorced families have to depend on the good will of parents for contact with their grandchildren?'. Zoe's father, who had been married three times before, had obviously thought about this but he, like other parents and grandparents in the group, seemed to believe, erroneously, that grandparents have a legal right to maintain contact with their grandchildren.

> It affects grandparents worse than it affects anybody else because they're not in control of anything, just going along with things. I know they have rights but it's a big problem because they don't think that they do have any rights. They sort of tend to step back and let a man and a woman sort their marital problems out and they get left by the wayside, which is a shame. (Zoe's father)

Interviews with members of the Grandparents' Association

Twelve interviews were carried out with members of the Grandparents' Association in the pilot phase of our study. Nine of these interviews were conducted by telephone and grandparents were simply asked to describe their family situation and to explain why they had been deprived of contact with their grandchildren. Clearly, members of the Association represent a very small and particular segment of the grandparenting population, but the interviews provided vivid testimony of the destructive effects of the hostilities that can accompany family disputes.

Grandparents' Association members suggested that a few ill-chosen words in defence of their divorced son or daughter or just a failure to give moral support to a daughter-in-law could be sufficient to cause a rift. Worried grandparents who voiced their fears about a resident parent's drug-taking or child abuse and those who talked to social services because they were tormented by their knowledge of the erratic and violent behaviour of a mother's new partner, lost contact with their grandchildren. They explained that they were reluctant to ask the court for permission to seek a contact order because of the deleterious effects that this might have on already damaged family relationships. One grandparent couple, who did attempt to take legal action, found that their grandchild had been persuaded to write to them refusing to see them again. The distress that cases of this kind caused meant that some grandparents and parents became locked into fierce and sometimes expensive battles that were unlikely to end happily for the grandchildren or for any of those involved.

One maternal grandmother reported that a failure to visit her grandchildren for several months because of work pressures led to a total ban on contact. Another maternal grandmother told us that she had suffered the same fate because she returned late from a day out with her grandchild. A paternal grandmother (who was unable to rely on her son for contact) discovered that trimming her granddaughter's hair had made her ex-daughter-in-law so angry that she was prevented from seeing her granddaughter. Such indiscretions could destroy already difficult relationships and separate grandparents from their grandchildren for a decade or more. Grandparents often interpreted these actions as cruel and high-handed and some believed that parents had become unreasonably jealous because their grandchild enjoyed the company of their grandparents.

Grandparents who could no longer see their grandchildren sometimes kept diaries in the hope that the grandchildren would one day read them and come to understand that their grandparents cared about them. Money was saved in the grandchild's name as an expression of love that parents could not undermine. Grandparents hoped that the cheques or bank accounts that were to be given to their grandchildren on their 18th birthdays would let them know that they had grandparents who cared about them. Birthday cards and presents were intercepted and thrown away before they could be opened and in one household children were disciplined for phoning their grandparents after the forbidden telephone number was spotted on the itemised bill.

It was difficult for these grandparents to come to terms with a system that seemed to them to recognise a parent's right to separate them from their grandchildren. It was particularly painful for those grandparents who had previously had close relationships with grandchildren. They were sure that their grandchildren would miss them and not understand why they their grandparents did not see them anymore.

Concluding comments

It can be questioned whether the law has much of a part to play in the kinds of family feuds that members of the Grandparents' Association described in their interviews. It is not immediately obvious how new family rights legislation would improve the situation of excluded grandparents. It could be argued that parents' duty to protect younger children means that they should normally retain the right to decide who should be allowed to build close relationships with their offspring. We must consider, therefore, whether it is appropriate to provide a right of contact to one category of family member that might prove to be distressing to the resident parent and disruptive to the child. Grandparents should perhaps respect the privacy of the nuclear family and obey the requirements of the 'norm of non-interference'. They should not therefore become involved unless invited to do so.

Some parents and grandparents in the study believed that grandparents were entitled by law to a relationship with their grandchildren. This erroneous belief was helpful on occasions in giving paternal grandparents the confidence to assert 'their rights' and persuade mothers to be more flexible. It might be extrapolated that the express grant of 'rights' might change attitudes in ways that can permeate through society and, in time, alter the climate of opinion.

For example, laws about race relations do not just ensure that those guilty of racism can be prosecuted but contribute to changes in the climate of opinion that might not otherwise have occurred. The recognition of grandparents' rights might also change thinking. They could enhance grandparents' status within families and eventually influence the feelings of the general population about the importance of grandparenting. However, apart from the objection that the mere proclamation of a 'right' does not in itself alter anyone's behaviour or thinking, or of itself improve the outcomes for children (King and Piper 1995), it cannot be *assumed* that the grandparent–grandchild relationship is a valuable resource for children without taking account of the nature and quality of the particular relationships in the individual family, and these must be judged on their merits.

We have suggested earlier in this book (Chapter Three) that grandparents' attitudes and approaches to grandparenting can often be traced to patterns of grandparenting behaviour that were established before the parents divorced. The nature of the grandparent–grandchild relationship before the break-up of the family, it was argued, was the main determinant of the post-divorce relationship. In this chapter, we have addressed an apparent contradiction. The fact that some grandparents become excluded appears to be evidence (in a minority of cases at least) that divorce *can* have a dramatic impact, particularly on paternal grandparents' relationships with their grandchildren. While this is undoubtedly true, it needs to be recalled that the excluded grandparents, interviewed in this study, either had a history of acrimonious relationships with their son or ex-daughter-in-law, or had been deprived of contact because of unresolved conflicts between the parents. Would the addition of further 'rights' assertions into such situations be likely to improve family harmony? It is a question to which we will return in the final chapter where we describe our conclusions about the public policy and legal issues that are most relevant to grandparenting in divorced families.

TWELVE

Conclusions: grandparents and family policy

The findings

Our study discovered that grandparents, parents and children often viewed grandparenting from very different perspectives. The role is extraordinarily diverse and the extent of that diversity in a sample of 44 families was surprising. When we came to consider the effects of divorce on the grandparent–grandchild relationship, we discovered that grandparents' approaches and attitudes to grandparenting usually survived the impact of divorce. We concluded that the evidence of continuities in grandparents' pre- and post-divorce behaviour was more compelling than the evidence of change as the result of family break-up. However, maternal grandparents often experienced an intensification of their childcare role and some paternal grandparents discovered that contact after divorce was more difficult or, in some cases, no longer possible.

Four 'continua' proved helpful in our reflections about grandparents' attitudes, functions and behaviour:

- Our exploration of the 'partisan–non-partisan' continuum provided evidence of the strength of grandparents' feelings. Strong emotions were generated by their sense of outrage at the way their adult child had been treated by their ex-spouse. Non-partisan grandparents saw that support for their ex-son or daughter-in-law could be exchanged for a long-term guarantee of future contact with their grandchildren and some felt strong ties of affection with their ex-child-in-law that they were unwilling to break.
- The 'enthusiastic–reluctant' continuum emphasised the diversity of grandparents' opinions. It highlighted the difference between those who wished to minimise their grandparenting role and were not afraid to say so, and those who saw grandparenting as a very significant phase of the life course and an important part of their day-to-day lives. Evidence from parents and grandchildren suggested that attitudes to grandparenting generally had origins that pre-dated family break-up.
- The 'adult-centred–child-centred' continuum was helpful in reminding us that the parenting of an adult child can be an important aspect of a grandparent's role. Some of the grandparents who were interviewed saw their adult child rather than their grandchild as their priority. Some grandchildren felt bored when grandparents devoted most of their attention

to the parent and expected them to amuse themselves during visits to their grandparents' house.

* Finally, the 'grandparent-as-parent–grandparent-as-grandparent' continuum drew attention to the differences that responsibility for childcare can make to grandparents. Evidence of pre- and post-divorce continuities in grandparenting behaviour again emerged. We discovered that paternal grandparents in divorced families who were much involved with their grandchildren before family break-up often became 'substitute parents' after the divorce. We interviewed maternal grandparents who were burdened by their responsibilities and some who felt that their role as substitute parents had taken away the fun of being a grandparent. 'Fun-seeking', we discovered, was a particularly desirable role for many grandparents and one that was popular with their grandchildren. It was a characteristic that was more common at the 'grandparent-as-grandparent' end of the continuum.

Three norms were discussed. The norms of 'non-interference' and 'obligation' have been frequently discussed in the grandparenting literature (see Chapter Two of this book). To these we added the 'norm of non-communication'. It might be expected that a lack of communication is undesirable but non-communication enabled parents, grandparents and children to respect boundaries, avoid sensitive or painful topics and support children's desire to remain loyal to both sides of their divorced family.

The study also examined the roles of grandmothers and grandfathers and maternal and paternal grandparents and explored some possible reasons for a 'grandparenting hierarchy of importance' (maternal grandmothers at the top, paternal grandfathers at the bottom). We investigated the reasons why maternal grandparents and maternal grandmothers in particular were often identified by parents as the 'main' or 'principal grandparent' and noted that maternal grandparents are at an advantage because of their close ties with their daughter. However, cultural expectations about appropriate roles for maternal and paternal grandparents may also be important. The expectation that paternal grandparents in divorced families will assume a less significant role may not be imposed by mothers and maternal grandparents; rather, it may be a perception that is also shared by paternal grandparents. There was a consensus in most parents' and grandparents' views about discipline but this might be explained by the fact that grandparents usually felt obliged to observe parents' wishes. Mothers often did not know much about their children's contact with their paternal grandparents, but were usually happy to accept that grandparents on either side of the family would need to reprimand their grandchildren on occasions. Grandparents often admitted that they had a favourite grandchild who might or might not be in the divorced family. Parents sometimes suspected this but did not want their children to be made aware of it and emphasised the importance of 'equal treatment' by grandparents of grandchildren.

The children who were interviewed generally believed that they had close relationships with their grandparents. The grandparent–grandchild relationship is often a positive and significant one for grandparents and grandchildren and this study has commented on the affection that grandparents and grandchildren shared and the practical help that grandparents provided for the wider family. However, among older grandchildren, assertions about close relationships were often accompanied by evidence of reduced contact. Older children saw less of their grandparents because they had begun to concentrate on peers, schoolwork and activities that took them away from the home. Older grandparents were sometimes perceived as 'old-fashioned' and 'out of touch' but, as we discovered, the generation gap is not always easily bridged. The picture that emerged in this study was distinctly mixed; consequently, we are inclined to agree with Finch (1989) that the grandparent–grandchild relationship is often more important to grandparents than to their grandchildren and is 'asymmetrical'.

The relevance to family policy and the law

This chapter's main aim is to consider whether or not the findings of our study lead to the conclusion that grandparenting should become an important strand in government thinking about family policy and the law. We have identified five key findings that seem likely to be relevant to grandparents and helpful in informing the policy debate.

1. *Finance.* There can be financial costs involved in being a grandparent in a divorced family. Many grandparents, we found, helped with housing, provided temporary accommodation, paid bills and provided loans and gifts of money for divorced parents. They also, on occasions, provided temporary accommodation for their adult sons and daughters and worked without payment to provide the childcare that allowed resident parents to go out to work. Is this purely a 'private matter' or an issue that deserves wider attention from the state?
2. *Improving the quality of grandparenting.* Some grandparents preferred a passive role and were described in this study as 'reluctant' grandparents. They had 'served their time' as parents and had no strong desire to become more involved with their children's families. They often had other interests and preferred to avoid demands that would disturb the established pattern of their lives. Could grandparents, either enthusiastic or reluctant, be helped to become 'better grandparents', who are more skilled at meeting their grandchildren's needs?
3. *Non-communication.* Some families appeared to cope with the pain of divorce with a strategic use of non-communication. Parents delayed telling their own parents about their decision to separate; grandchildren did not usually talk to their grandparents about their parents' divorce, and parents often knew very little about their child's relationship with their ex-spouse's family. Children learned to be discreet and remained loyal to both parents. Grandparents learned not to ask questions about children's contact with the

'other side' of the divorced family. Does this represent a problem that needs to be tackled and, if so, how should it be addressed?

4. *Grandparents and the law.* This study gathered information about family conflicts that led to a rift in relationships with grandparents. We also investigated the feelings of loss that occur when grandparents are permanently separated from their grandchildren (see Chapter Eleven). Our grandparent group made almost no use of the legal system to seek redress for their grievances. However, it was wrongly assumed, in a few cases, that grandparents have rights. Is the current legal position, in which grandparents are neither granted a right of contact nor excused from the requirement to seek the court's permission before applying for a contact order, in the best interests of families?

5. *Contact and childcare.* The generous help and support that some grandparents provided for their families after parental divorce were, as we discovered, occasionally burdensome. There is a need to balance the interests of parents and grandchildren with those of grandparents who, without explicit negotiation, can become their grandchildren's long-term, daytime carers. Is it in the interests of both parents and grandparents in divorced families to encourage grandparents to provide significant amounts of childcare support? Or is it in the interests of the state? Furthermore, should reluctant grandparents be persuaded to become more involved with their grandchildren?

Finance: payments for childcare

Given grandparents' contribution to the welfare of families, it is now appropriate to ask whether grandparents should be paid for supporting their families (Richards, 2001; Arthur et al, 2002). It would be uncontroversial to suggest that grandparents who *replace* parents and provide full-time care for their grandchildren should be supported with money and sources of help and advice that would have otherwise been available to the children's parents. Richards and Tapsfield (2003) have provided a clear account of how this might be achieved.

It is more controversial, however, to ask whether the tax and benefits system should be changed to ensure that some financial support is channelled to grandparents who are *not* solely responsible for bringing up their grandchildren but who do, nevertheless, have major childcare responsibilities. Grandparents who care for children and allow a single parent to go to work may be responsible for creating a tax-paying employee and reducing the obligations of the benefits system to provide financial support for the family. They may also be indirectly responsible for preventing their grandchildren from living in poverty: their dedicated service is not only of benefit to the family but also of benefit to the state. It is difficult to envisage how government payments to these grandparents could be managed when it would be all too easy for mothers to declare that their parents were providing essential childcare, whether this was the case or not.

Arthur et al (2002) interviewed parents and grandparents, and investigated their feelings about payments for childcare. Some of their respondents pointed out that it would be difficult to avoid a situation in which people cheated the system by exaggerating the amount of care they provided. The report also looked at the suggestion that parents rather than the public purse should assume responsibility for paying grandparents. There was a strong tendency for the grandparents in Arthur et al's study to say that they would never accept payments from their own children. They were worried that "receiving money would turn grandparenting into a job" (Arthur et al, 2002, p 76) and that this would alter the nature of family relationships and perhaps cause parents to become resentful. Furthermore, when Perry et al (2000) investigated the effects of marriage breakdown on family finances, they discovered that 43% of divorced mothers with children reported that they had experienced times when they had been unable to cope financially. Divorced mothers may be in greater financial difficulties than their parents and may well have had to ask them for financial support. Paying grandparents is probably much cheaper than paying for nursery provision, but it would be difficult for grandparents who were aware of their child's financial problems to accept payments for childcare. No doubt, some families may make regular 'gifts' to grandparents to show their appreciation for the help that they have received. Some parents and grandparents, however, may feel uncomfortable with such arrangements.

There must also be concerns about whether payments for childcare would make grandparents employees of their own children, and whether or not employment law would need to be observed. Would the payments from parent to grandparent be taxable or affect grandparents' entitlements to state benefits? The 'wage-for-childcare' route seems fraught with complications whether the payments are made by the state or paid by sons and daughters. It seems sensible to conclude that it will not become a serious option except for grandparents who have assumed full responsibility for their grandchildren. It is unlikely to become part of government policy particularly as grandparents themselves (see Arthur et al, 2002, p 75) have expressed a reluctance about accepting payments. We are indebted to Professor Hilary Land, however, for pointing out that while notions of payment for grandparents may be problematic, the idea of 'reimbursement' for loss can be a helpful concept. This may be particularly pertinent for grandparents in divorced families who give up work to allow the resident parent to seek employment. In these circumstances, enhancement of pension rights could be justified and the government could allow grandparents to make such an application. This form of recompense would not be a 'wage' but a compensation payment or 'reimbursement' for a loss incurred as a result of the grandparents' decision to provide essential support for their grandchildren.

Improving the quality of grandparenting

As we have discovered in this study, there are grandparents who are unsure of their grandparenting role and not good at relating to children. Some of these grandparents may be interested in opportunities to learn new grandparenting skills. There are three ways in which such opportunities could be provided:

- grandparenting training courses;
- improved access to professional help that could be given directly or provided through an advice line staffed by experts in childcare (Home Office, 1998);
- further development of the work of the grandparent organisations with government help in providing these services. Should those in government and elsewhere want to mobilise grandparents and encourage them to accept more responsibility for their grandchildren's upbringing, more resources would be needed to support programmes of advice and training.

We begin with a discussion of the place of training programmes and go on to consider the place of professional support and advice and the part that the voluntary organisations play.

Training programmes

Szinovacz and Roberts (1998) and Robertson et al (1985) are among those in the US who have made proposals about the content of training programmes for grandparents. Szinovacz and Roberts note that training programmes can be aimed at improving the quality of grandparenting, the provision of support for grandparents who are bringing up their grandchildren, or more generally concerned with improving intergenerational relationships in the community. Adult education classes in Britain could cover such topics as managing adolescents, coping with children's worries after parental divorce, helping grandchildren with the National Curriculum, playing with young children, drug abuse and child discipline. Richards recommends the development of programmes for grandparent carers "that could include information and advice on managing relationships between the generations, coping with young children and teenagers, financial issues and support with education and health needs" (2001, p 105). Strom and Strom (1991) argue that grandparents in the US should consider whether they have fallen behind the times, are out of touch with new technology and are prone to outmoded moral precepts and expectations about standards of behaviour. In our study, we identified grandparents who were perceived by their adult children and grandchildren to be impatient, out of touch and 'old-fashioned'. Some of these grandparents were also 'reluctant grandparents' and willing to admit this. Strom and Strom's programme would attempt to teach them permissiveness, tolerance, flexible attitudes, respect for individuality and the value of lifelong education.

It is difficult to know how programmes to improve grandparenting skills would be greeted by British grandparents and whether or not a sufficient number would be willing to attend in order to make them viable. There would undoubtedly be scepticism and some grandparents might suspect that they were being asked to 'go back to school' and might worry that the experience would leave them exposed and vulnerable to ridicule. More confident grandparents might feel that their long experience of bringing up children had taught them all they needed to know. Strom and Strom (1991) recount a story about a grandmother who wondered why she needed to attend a grandparenting course. She challenged the authors by remarking, "I raised three children. All of them turned out OK, so I must have known something" (see page 3). Grandparents might feel that it would be presumptuous for 'experts' to tell them how to behave, particularly when their approach to childcare is something that needs to reflect the values of their own family and, since grandparenting is a 'mediated' activity (see Chapter Two of this book), the parent's wishes. However, training courses could be useful to provide grandparents with opportunities to discuss the grandparent–grandchild relationship. How many would want to change their behaviour if they were aware that their grandchild was bored during their visits? Would some want to reflect on their adult-centred approach, become more 'fun-seeking' or less partisan in their behaviour? It could be helpful for some grandparent couples to learn about the general differences in grandmothers' and grandfathers' relationships with their grandchildren, to become aware of the impact of family conflict, and understand more about children's feelings of loyalty to the non-resident parent and their paternal grandparents. Moreover, grandparents with major childcare responsibilities would probably have a great deal to learn from each other's experience, although this kind of provision could be made through support groups (see page 138).

Support and advice from the professionals

There are sources of advice from professionals from which grandparents could benefit without the need to enrol on a formal programme of grandparent training. Social workers, health visitors, family doctors and teachers, for example, can be asked for their advice and both a 'helpline' and a network of family 'advice surgeries' (Home Office, 1998, p 10) have emerged as elements of government strategy for family support. Richards (2001, p 105) and the Home Office (1998) both recommend that professionals should be encouraged to respond to grandparents' needs for advice and take much more account of the contribution that they make to the welfare of the wider family. However, many grandparents will decide that it is inappropriate to seek the advice of social workers or health visitors: parents may react negatively to any suggestion that grandparents should seek professional help or attend advice clinics. Even when grandparents play a major role in helping to care for grandchildren, this does not reduce the possibility of family conflict when a grandparent is deemed to have infringed the norm of non-interference. Grandparents often find themselves walking a fine line between support and interference and seeking advice from professionals is a route that contains traps for the unwary.

Support groups

Support groups, discussion groups and programmes that grandparents and grandchildren can attend together can combat isolation and provide grandparents with opportunities to learn from each other and from visiting professionals. The grandparent and toddler playgroups of the kind that the Grandparents' Association is currently pioneering are a good example of a scheme that promises to support children while helping grandparents to cope with their own concerns and their need for advice. Imaginative schemes that provide the same kinds of support for the grandparents of school-age children and young teenagers are also needed. Silverstein and Vehvilainen (2000) suggested that grandparents' participation in school and in after-school activities could be beneficial. Their comments were aimed at grandparents who had assumed full responsibility for grandchildren; however, they could equally be applied to grandparents in general. There are particular strengths of approaches that either involve grandparents and grandchildren working together or that allow grandparents to discuss grandparenting with other experienced grandparents. These approaches can cater for grandparents' needs without directly indicating the need for interventions, which would make many parents feel uneasy. There is an important difference between seeking advice about a particular grandchild (which could be interpreted as interference) and learning about grandparenting in the company of other grandparents.

However, organisations such as the Grandparents' Association are often aimed at grandparents who have serious problems or who are facing difficult situations that are, thankfully, outside the experience of most people. Those who have been deprived of contact with their grandchildren and those who are their grandchildren's full-time carers account for almost all of the membership of the Grandparents' Association. It is highly probable that their decision to join the organisation was prompted by their pressing needs for support and advice. Most grandparents who see themselves as 'ordinary' (and this includes most grandparents in divorced families) do not become members of grandparenting groups although many would surely benefit from the experience.

The value of 'collective struggle' (Cohen and Pyle, 2000), of networking and acquiring a sense of community seems to be taken much more seriously in the US than in the UK. Kornhaber (1996), for example, believes passionately in the Intergenerational Movement in the US. He explains that it aims to extend the benefits of good grandparenting into the community through:

> activities, programs and events that form relationships and involve co-operation between generations. Programs geared to youths under 25 and elders over 60 years of age are being established all over the country. (Kornhaber, 1996, p 193)

The grandparent organisations in the UK, and the networks of support groups that they have developed, allow people to share experiences and recognise that the challenges they face are not unique. They provide opportunities for their members to exchange views, learn from each other's experience, seek advice and draw on the expertise of a trained group leader. They have social functions too, because they bring like-minded people together and may lead to the development of friendships that thrive outside group meetings. These groups occasionally attract practitioners from a range of fields that members would not otherwise have an opportunity to meet. They can use their collective energies to improve public awareness of the issues that affect them and act politically in the hope of obtaining changes in legislation or concessions from government that serve their members' interests. Support groups are relatively cheap to run, cost little to join and are capable of giving grandparents a 'sense of belonging' and the pleasurable experience of giving and receiving help from others who share their concerns. Their continued expansion may depend, however, on their ability to appeal to 'ordinary' grandparents as well as those who have considerable problems with issues of contact and care.

Policy and the 'norm of non-communication'

The position of many counsellors and family therapists is that the solution to family problems begins by letting family members know how everyone thinks and feels. The counsellor's role is often to facilitate the communication process or, as Street (1994, p 89) explained, is like "oiling a rusty bicycle" or "lubricating the family's interaction about the topic at hand".

> The counsellor acts as a channel aiming to 'hear' the views of everyone. In the early stages of counselling, the family will not 'hear' in the empathic sense, but the counsellor will be ensuring that the clogged channels of the family's communication mechanisms are being slowly and gently unblocked, especially by reflecting feelings and thoughts. (Street, 1994, p 89)

The view that a counsellor's contribution is to free 'clogged channels' and 'lubricate rusty mechanisms' seems to suggest that communications that were once in good order have somehow fallen into disrepair. However, in this study, the descriptions that parents, grandparents and children gave of their family's avoidance of open discussion did not seem to be the result of negligence or neglect but matters of policy and strategy. Families in our study used non-communication (which can be interpreted as 'respect for boundaries') to avoid causing pain. Reimers (1999), a family therapist, is among those who clearly recognise the problem and has noted that clients avoid highly charged issues by changing the subject, by the use of non-sequiturs, and strategies that avoid encounters with emotional intensity.

We can all sense danger in the face of questions even when none is intended. Within close relationships there are many questions which can feel dangerous or impossible to answer straightforwardly. (Reimers, 1999, p 364)

There are risks in communicating openly about sensitive topics and the decision to keep relationships with both sides of the family separate from one another may have been wise. We concluded that the grandparents, parents and children in the divorced families in our study had learned that 'non-communication' can be a valuable coping strategy. It is a possibility that is not fully recognised in the traditional approach of family therapists and counsellors and one that might be considered by those court officers and others who are responsible for liaising with separated couples and their families. Grandparents should also be deterred from believing that they are automatically cast in the role of family counsellors or confidants in divorced families or that children should be pressed for information that they may not wish to divulge. It may be true that divorced mothers who use high levels of 'avoidant coping' (including non-communication) experience higher levels of psychological distress in the long run (Tein et al, 2000). However, counsellors and mediators should be wary of treating a lack of emotional openness as unfortunate and necessarily in need of immediate correction without recognising its value to members of divorced families. This may be particularly important in family therapy when an ill-advised sharing of information may have adverse effects on the long-term development of relationships.

Family law and excluded grandparents

In Chapter Seven of this book, the possibility of English law providing grandparents with automatic standing in litigation over the right to contact with grandchildren was discussed. We considered why grandparents should be required to seek the leave of the court before being allowed to apply for a contact order, and raised the issue of resident parents who simply ignored court orders that grandparents had won as a result of expensive litigation. Since our study did not focus on families in conflict, it is not surprising that few of the grandparents had had any direct involvement in legal proceedings. In this respect, our sample of grandparents is different from other previous socio-legal studies that have deliberately concentrated on grandparents who *have* had to resort to the courts, or who have tried and failed to seek legal remedies when parents have opposed their attempts to enjoy contact with their grandchildren (Douglas and Lowe, 1990; Kaganas and Piper, 1990; Drew, 2000). This study suggests that, in most divorced families, the relationship between the grandparents, parents and grandchildren is negotiated, maintained or diminished without reference to the possible legal position. It was only when grandparents felt that the post-divorce relationship did not reflect that which they enjoyed prior to the breakdown that a real sense of grievance came to the fore. In such cases, the cost of legal action and the fear of making matters worse deterred grandparents from resorting to the courts. Should it be made easier, then, for these grandparents to seek court orders to require parents with care to allow contact with grandchildren?

The leave requirement is criticised by grandparent lobbyists (see Chapter Seven) because it is believed to place an unfair hurdle in the way of grandparents. The contrary argument is to point out that it is only in a minority of cases that grandparents are being treated 'unfairly' by the resident parent, in relation to the prior situation that existed between them. In such cases, they will easily obtain leave, and it is better to require them to do so than to place all post-divorce families at risk of substantive legal proceedings being brought by grandparents regardless of the nature and quality of their prior relationships. Those lobbying for grandparents to have express 'rights' argue that what grandparents want is recognition that they are in a special position regarding their grandchildren which should be reflected by the law vesting them with automatic rights to contact and to seek care. Our study does not support this view. It shows that the range of grandparenting styles, and the diversity in the quality of family relationships across the generations, refutes the suggestion that the fact of being a grandparent is enough, per se, to justify special recognition.

We agree with Lussier et al (2002, p 375) who argue that judges cannot order "harmonious, supportive family relationships" and that "family-generated compromise through the process of mediation" provides the most promising prospects for resolving conflict. As long as it remains the general view that courts are not the best places in which to resolve family disputes, it would seem unwise to single out grandparents as a group deserving extra help in invoking the legal process. The language of 'rights' has become more prevalent since the 1998 Human Rights Act. It is premature, however, in the light of current European human rights jurisprudence, to conclude that this has strengthened the claims of grandparents. The present study confirms, in our view, that the current legal position in both domestic and human rights law correctly requires grandparents to justify their claim to legal protection on the basis of the actual relationship they have had with their grandchildren rather than on the basis of their 'status' as grandparents alone.

Childcare: contact and the 'burden' of care

At the heart of the grandparenting policy debate are questions about how grandparents can be helped and encouraged to offer *more* support to the wider family. The Home Office puts the issue plainly, stating: "We also intend to help grandparents and older people offer more support to families" (Home Office, 1998, p 5, section 1.5). Grandparents usually want to meet parents' expectations and those of society and to feel that they have earned the right to view their grandparenting role with a sense of satisfaction. Contact with grandchildren is very important and, as we discovered, grandparents do not abandon hope in the face of difficult circumstances but 'play for the long term' by employing strategies to secure their contact or restore it at some time in the distant future.

This is why some paternal grandparents, whose divorced sons could only provide unreliable access to their grandchildren, covered all eventualities by maintaining good relationships with both parents. It also explains why paternal grandparents, who quarrel with their son, offer support to their ex-daughter-in-law to secure contact and why those excluded grandparents who kept diaries and saved money for their grandchild's 18th birthday might also be seen as 'long term players'. They imagined that young adults might assert their independence, become free from parental restrictions and want to restore their relationship with their grandparents. It also explains why a grandmother might 'selectively invest' in grandchildren who seem to provide good prospects of a long and satisfying relationship (see Cherlin and Furstenberg, 1985; Chapter Two of this book). It would be interesting to know what happens in these cases over time and whether or not contact between grandparents and their adult grandchildren is, in fact, re-established.

Contact with children and grandchildren provides an opportunity for some grandparents to become part of family life and to be stimulated by their re-involvement. The most important benefit for many grandparents is that they are repaid in love, or what Cherlin and Furstenberg (1992) have called 'sentimental currency'. Grandparents, they suggested, can "bask in what they perceive as the special achievements of their grandchildren". However, these authors echoed a view that emerged from this study when they added, "When our respondents told us about their strong feelings for their grandchildren, we sometimes sensed reservations about whether the feelings were reciprocated" (Cherlin and Furstenberg, 1992, p 195).

Most grandparents would no doubt firmly reject the idea that their strong desire for regular contact leaves them open to exploitation by their sons and daughters. But some dedicated maternal grandparents in our study were providing support for their children and grandchildren on a daily basis. The tension between their sense of family obligation and their regret at their loss of freedom emerged during their interviews (see Chapter Ten). It appeared that they wanted to be with their grandchildren as often as possible but, in truth, they were also regretting the loss of their freedom in retirement and some felt under considerable strain. They wanted an emotionally satisfying grandchild–grandparent relationship – but discovered that they had taken on a parental role. The 'fun' of being a grandparent had been displaced by responsibilities that they would have preferred in smaller measure. Although the grandparenting phase in life might have been eagerly anticipated, some grandparents found themselves taking an unexpected backward step when they became 'parent-like' grandparents with all the responsibilities that this implied.

This suggests that policy reform cannot just be aimed at ensuring that grandparents are encouraged to do more and more to support their families. One of the dangers of researchers' and policy makers' current interest in grandparenting is that it will add to the already considerable moral pressure on grandparents. The fact that some grandparents are over-committed may simply be a symptom of a lack of other options for mothers who wish to return to work. The Home Office (1998) consultation paper, *Supporting families*, makes it clear that the government wants to provide better services to support lone parents who want to work (Home Office, 1998, p 18). As part of its 1998 childcare strategy the UK government promised to provide another million childcare places by 2004 and Green Papers were published in Scotland (The Stationery Office, May 1998) and in Wales (Welsh Office, June 1998). All four-year-olds were given access to at least a part-time pre-school place and plans were made to extend this provision to all three-year-olds while enhancing the range of childcare options available to parents. In 2002, however, the Day Care Trust reported (see *The Guardian*, 6 February 2002) that British parents faced the highest childcare bills in Europe; that progress towards the million extra places had been slow, and that demand for childcare outstripped supply. Tributes to the dedicated service of loving grandparents should not distract ministers from recognising that the need for a large investment in affordable childcare is overdue.

Concluding comments

The parents whom we met in the course of our research usually depended on their own parents for childcare support and some had become almost entirely dependent on daily help from their children's grandparents. When grandparents live nearby, have close relationships with the resident parent, are in good health and enjoy being re-involved in family life, they may represent a solution to the family's childcare problems that parents know they can trust. However, these ideal conditions do not always exist and, even when they do, grandparents should not feel trapped by their willingness to help. If families are to be allowed the childcare of their choice, then accessible, affordable and high quality alternatives must be made available.

Grandparents, especially those who have sacrificed some of the joys of grandparenthood to assume major childcare duties on behalf of their divorced adult child, are fulfilling their grandparenting role in a way that benefits their families, their communities and the state. Policies and services to support them need to be understood in the light of the feelings of grandchildren and parents as well as those of grandparents themselves. As family break-up becomes more common, it is important to understand the intricacy of grandparent–grandchild relationships in divided families and how best to balance the interests of family members. This study has illustrated the diversity of grandparenting and the variety of family relationships that must be taken into account. It is hoped that the evidence here will increase understanding of contemporary grandparenting in the UK and provide a stepping-stone to future research that emphasises the internal dynamics of the relationship and describes the nature of grandparenting over time and in a variety of cultures and social settings.

References

Advisory Board on Family Law: Children Act Sub-Committee (2002) *Making contact work*, London: Lord Chancellor's Department.

Aldous, J. (1985) 'Parent–adult child relations as affected by the grandparent status', in V.L. Bengtson and J.F. Robertson (eds) *Grandparenthood*, Beverly Hills, CA: Sage Publications.

Aldous, J. (1995) 'New views of grandparents in intergenerational context', *Journal of Family Issues*, vol 16, no 1, pp 104-22.

Allen, K.R., Blieszner, R. and Roberto, K.A. (2000) 'Families in the middle and later years: a review and critique of research in the 1990s', *Journal of Marriage and the Family*, vol 62, pp 911-26.

Amato, P.R. and Keith, B. (1991) 'Parental divorce and the well being of children: a meta-analysis', *Psychological Bulletin*, vol 110, no 1, pp 26-46.

Aquilino, W.S. (1999) 'Two views on one relationship: comparing parents' and young adult children's reports on the quality of intergenerational relations', *Journal of Marriage and the Family*, vol 61, no 4, pp 858-70.

Arthur, S., Snape, D. and Dench, G. (2002) 'The moral economy of grandparenting', Unpublished report prepared for the Nuffield Foundation and the Institute of Community Studies.

Beck, U. and Beck-Gernsheim, E. (2002) *Individualisation*, London: Sage Publications.

Bengtson, V.L. (1985) 'Diversity and symbolism in grandparental roles', in V. Bengtson and J.F. Robertson (eds) *Grandparenthood*, Beverly Hills, CA: Sage Publications.

Bengtson, V.L. (2001) 'Beyond the nuclear family: the increasing importance of multigenerational bonds', *Journal of Marriage and the Family*, vol 63, pp 1-16.

Boszormenghnagy, I. and Spark, G. (1973) *Invisible loyalties*, New York, NY: Harper and Row.

Brown, J. and Day-Sclater, S. (1999) 'Divorce: a psychodynamic perspective', in S. Day-Sclater and C. Piper (eds) *Undercurrents of divorce*, Aldershot: Ashgate.

Burghes, L., Clarke, L. and Cronin, N. (1997) *Fathers and fatherhood in Britain*, Occasional Paper 23, London: Family Policy Studies Centre.

Burton, L.M. and Bengtson, V.L. (1985) 'Black grandmothers: issues of timing and continuity of roles', in V.L. Bengtson and J.F. Robertson (eds) *Grandparenthood*, Beverly Hills, CA: Sage Publications.

Chadwick-Jones, J.K. (1976) *Social exchange theory: Its structure and influence in social psychology*, London: Academic Press.

Chan, C.G. and Elder, G.H. (2000) 'Matrilineal advantage in grandchild–grandparent relations', *The Gerontologist*, vol 40, pp 179-90.

Cherlin, A. and Furstenberg, F.F. (1985) 'Styles and strategies of grandparenting', in V.L. Bengtson and J.F. Robertson (eds) *Grandparenthood*, Beverly Hills, CA: Sage Publications.

Cherlin, A.J. and Furstenberg, F.F. (1992) *The new American grandparent*, Cambridge, MA: Harvard University Press.

Clingempeel, W.G., Colyar, J.J., Brand, E. and Hetherington, E.M. (1992) 'Children's relationships with maternal grandparents: a longitudinal study of family structure and pubertal status effects', *Child Development*, vol 63, pp 1404-22.

Cohen, C.S. and Pyle, R.P. (2000) 'Support groups in the lives of grandmothers raising grandchildren', in B. Cox (ed) *To grandmother's house we go and stay: Perspectives on custodial grandparents*, New York, NY: Springer Publishing Company.

Cooney, T.M. and Smith, A.L. (1996) 'Young adults' relations with grandparents following recent parental divorce', *Journal of Gerontology: Social Sciences*, vol 51, no 2, pp 91-5.

Cooney, T.M. and Uhlenberg, P. (1990) 'The role of divorce in men's relationships with adult children after mid-life', *Journal of Marriage and the Family*, vol 52, pp 677-88.

Creasey, G. (1993) 'The association between divorce and late adolescent grandchildren's relationships with grandparents', *Journal of Youth and Adolescence*, vol 22, pp 513-29.

Creasey, A.J. and Koblewski, P.J. (1991) 'Adolescent grandchildren's relationships with maternal and paternal grandmothers and grandfathers', *Journal of Adolescence*, vol 14, pp 373-87.

Crook, H. (2001) '*Troxel et vir v Granville*: grandparent visitation rights in the United States Supreme Court', *Child and Family Law Quarterly*, vol 13, no 1, pp 101-14.

Dench, G. and Ogg, J. (2002) *Grandparenting in Britain: A baseline study*, London: Institute of Community Studies.

Dench, G., Ogg, J. and Thomson, K. (1999) 'The role of grandparents', in R. Jowell, Curtice, J., Park, A. and Thomson, K. (eds) *British social attitudes: The 16th Report*, Aldershot: Ashgate and National Centre for Social Research.

Douglas, G. (2000) 'The family, gender and social security', in N. Harris (ed) *Social security law in context*, Oxford: Oxford University Press, pp 259-89.

Douglas, G. and Ferguson, N. (2003) 'The role of grandparents in divorced families', *The International Journal of Law, Policy and the Family*, vol 17, no 1, pp 41-67.

Douglas, G. and Lowe, N. (1990) 'Grandparents and the legal process', *Journal of Social Welfare Law*, vol 2, pp 98-106.

Douglas, G., Butler, I., Murch, M., Robinson, M. and Scanlan, L. (2000) 'Children's perspectives and experiences of the divorce process', Unpublished report prepared for the Economic and Social Research Council, Cardiff: Cardiff Family Studies Research Centre.

Douglas, G., Lowe, N., Murch, M., Robinson, M., Ferguson, N. and Bader, K. (2002) 'Grandparenting in a divorced family', Unpublished final report to the Nuffield Foundation.

Drew, L. (2000) 'Grandparents and divorce', *Journal of the British Society of Gerontology*, vol 3, pp 7-10.

Drew, L. and Smith, P.K. (1999) 'The impact of parental separation/divorce on grandparent–grandchild relationships', *The International Journal of Aging and Human Development*, vol 48, no 3, pp 191-216.

Drew, L. and Smith, P.K. (2002) 'Implications for grandparents when they lose contact with their grandchildren: divorce, family feud and geographical separation', *Journal of Mental Health and Aging*, vol 8, no 2, pp 95-119.

Drew, L., Richard, M. and Smith, P.K. (1998) 'Grandparenting and its relationship to parenting', *Clinical Child Psychology and Psychiatry*, vol 3, no 3, pp 465-80.

Dubas, S.D. (2001) 'How gender moderates the grandparent–grandchild relationship', *Journal of Family Issues*, vol 22, no 4, pp 478-92.

Dunn, J. and Deater-Deckard, K. (2001) *Children's views of their changing families*, York: Joseph Rowntree Foundation.

Dunn, J., Davies, L.C., O'Connor, T.G. and Sturges, W. (2001) 'Family lives and friendships: the perspectives of children in step-, single-parent and nonstep families', *Journal of Family Psychology*, vol 15, no 2, pp 272-87.

Eisenberg, A.R. (1988) 'Grandchildren's perspectives on relationships with grandparents: the influence of gender across generations', *Sex Roles*, vol 19, pp 205-17.

Family Policy Studies Centre (2000) 'Family change: a guide to the issues', Briefing Paper 12.

Ferri, E. and Smith, K. (1996) *Parenting in the 1990s*, London: Family Policy Studies Centre.

Finch, J. (1989) *Family obligations and social change*, Cambridge: Polity Press.

Findler, L.S. (2000) 'The role of grandparents in the social support system of mothers of children with a physical disability', *Families in Society: The Journal of Contemporary Human Services*, vol 81, no 4, pp 370-81.

Firth, R., Hubert, J. and Forge, A. (1970) *Families and their relatives*, London: Routledge and Kegan Paul.

Freud, S. (1910, 1912 and 1918) 'Essays on love', in J. Strachey, A. Freud, A. Strachey and A. Tyson (eds) (1995) *The complete psychological works of Sigmund Freud*, vol 11, London: Hogarth Press, pp 165-208.

Freud, S. (1913) 'Totem and taboo', in J. Strachey, A. Freud, A. Strachey, and A. Tyson (eds) (1995) *The complete psychological works of Sigmund Freud*, vol 13, London: Hogarth Press, pp 1-61.

Gesell, A. and Ilg, F.L. (1946) *The child from five to ten*, New York, NY: Harper and Row.

Gibson, P.A. (2002) 'African-American grandmothers as caregivers: answering the call to help their grandchildren', *Families in Society*, vol 83, no 1, pp 35-43.

Giddens, A. (1992) *The transformations of intimacy*, Cambridge: Polity Press.

Gladstone, J.W. (1989) 'Grandmother–grandchild contact: the mediating influence of the middle generation following marriage breakdown and remarriage', *Canadian Journal on Aging*, vol 8, pp 355-65.

Glaser, B. and Strauss, A. (1968) *The discovery of grounded theory*, London: Weidenfeld and Nicholson.

Hagestad, G.O. (1985) 'Continuity and connectedness', in V.L. Bengtson and J.F. Robertson (eds) *Grandparenthood*, Beverly Hills, CA: Sage Publications, pp 31-48.

Henricson, C. (2003) *Government and parenting*, York: Joseph Rowntree Foundation.

Hetherington, E.M. and Stanley-Hagan, M. (1999) 'The adjustment of children with divorced parents: a risk and resiliency perspective', *Journal of Child Psychology and Psychiatry*, vol 40, no 1, pp 129-40.

Hodgson, L.G. (1992) 'Adult grandchildren and their grandparents: the enduring bond', *International Journal of Aging and Human Development*, vol 34, no 3, pp 209-25.

Homans, G.C. (1961) *Social behaviour: Its elementary forms*, New York, NY: Harcourt, Brace and World.

Home Office (1998) *Supporting families: A consultation document*, London: The Stationery Office.

Hurme, H. (1991) 'Dimensions of the grandparent role in Finland', in P.K. Smith (ed) *The psychology of grandparenthood: An international perspective*, London: Routledge.

Jensen, A.-M. (2003) 'For the children's sake: symbolic power lost?', in A.-M. Jensen and L. McKee (eds) *Children and the changing family: Between transformation and negotiation*, London: Routledge Falmer.

Johnson, C. (1985) 'Grandparenting options in divorcing families: an anthropological perspective', in V.L. Bengtson and J.F. Robertson (eds) *Grandparenthood*, Beverley Hills, CA: Sage Publications.

Johnson, C. and Barer, B.M. (1987) 'Marital instability and the changing kinship networks of grandparents', *The Gerontologist*, vol 27, pp 330-5.

Johnson, C.L. (1998a) 'Effects of adult children's divorce on grandparenthood', in M.E. Szinovacz (ed) *Handbook on grandparenthood*, Connecticut, CT: Greenwood Press.

Johnson, C.L. (1998b) *Ex familia: Grandparents, parents and children adjust to divorce*, New Brunswick, NJ: Rutgers University Press.

Johnston, J. and Campbell, L. (1988) *The impasse of divorce: The dynamics and resolution of family conflict*, New York, NY: Free Press.

Kaganas, F. and Piper, C. (1990) 'Grandparents and the limits of the law', *International Journal of Law Policy and the Family*, vol 4, pp 27-51.

Kaganas, F. and Piper, C. (2001) 'Grandparents and contact: "Rights v Welfare" revisited', *International Journal of Law, Policy and the Family*, vol 15, no 2, pp 250-75.

Kennedy, G.E. (1992) 'Quality in grandparent–grandchild relationships', *International Journal of Aging and Human Development*, vol 35, pp 83-98.

King, M. and Piper, C. (1995) *How the law thinks about children* (2nd edn), Aldershot: Arena.

King, V. and Elder, G.H. (1997) 'The legacy of grandparenting: childhood experiences with grandparents and current involvement with grandchildren', *Journal of Marriage and the Family*, vol 59, pp 848-59.

Kivett, V.R. (1991) 'The grandparent–grandchild connection', *Marriage and Family Review*, vol 16, pp 267-90.

Kivett, V.R. (1993) 'Racial comparisons of the grandmother role: implications for strengthening the family support system of older black women', *Family Relations*, vol 42, pp 165-72.

Kivnick, H.Q. (1981) 'Grandparenthood and the mental health of grandparents', *Ageing and Society*, vol 1, no 3, pp 365-91.

Kivnick, H.Q. (1982) 'Grandparenthood: an overview of meaning and mental health', *The Gerontologist*, vol 22, pp 59-66.

Klein, D.M. and White, J.M. (1996) *Family theories: An introduction*, London: Sage Publications.

Komiya, N., Good, G. and Sherrod, N. (2000) 'Emotional openness as a predictor of college students' attitudes towards seeking psychological help', *Journal of Counselling Psychology*, vol 47, no 1, pp 138-43.

Kornhaber, A. (1996) *Contemporary grandparenting*, London: Sage Publications.

Kornhaber, A. and Woodward, K. (1981) *Grandparents–grandchildren: The vital connection*, New York, NY: Doubleday.

Kruk, E. and Hall, B.L. (1995) 'The disengagement of paternal grandparents subsequent to divorce', *Journal of Divorce and Remarriage*, vol 23, pp 131-47.

Law Commission (1988) *Review of child law: Guardianship and custody*, Report No 172, London: HMSO.

Lee, R.M. and Liu, H.T. (2001) 'Coping with intergenerational family conflict: comparison of Asian American, Hispanic and European American college students', *Journal of Counselling Psychology*, vol 48, no 4, pp 410-19.

Leek, M. and Smith, P.K. (1991) 'Cooperation and conflict in three-generation families', in P.K. Smith (ed) *The psychology of grandparenthood: An international perspective*, London: Routledge.

Lussier, G., Deater-Deckard, K., Dunn, J. and Davies, L. (2002) 'Support across two generations: children's closeness to grandparents following parental divorce and remarriage', *Journal of Family Psychology*, vol 16, pp 363-76.

McCready, M. (1985) 'Styles of grandparenting among white ethnics', in V.L Bengtson and J.F. Robertson (eds) *Grandparenthood*, Beverly Hills, CA: Sage Publications.

McLanahan, S. and Booth, A.K. (1989) 'Mother-only families: problems, prospects and politics', *Journal of Marriage and the Family*, vol 51, pp 557-80.

Matteson, J. and Babb, P. (eds) (2002) *Social trends 32*, London: The Stationery Office.

Matthews, S.H. and Sprey, J. (1984) 'The impact of divorce on grandparenthood: an exploratory study', *The Gerontologist*, vol 24, pp 41-7.

Matthews, S.H. and Sprey, J. (1985) 'Adolescents' relationships with grandparents: an empirical contribution to conceptual clarification', *Journal of Gerontology*, vol 40, no 5, pp 621-6.

Miles, B.M. and Huberman, A.M. (1994) *Qualitative data analysis*, London: Sage Publications.

Mills, T.L. (2001) 'Research on grandparent and grandchild relationships in the new millennium', *Journal of Family Issues*, vol 22, no 4, pp 403-6.

Mills, T.L., Wakeman, M.A. and Fea, C.B. (2001) 'Adult grandchildren's perceptions of emotional closeness and consensus with their maternal and paternal gramdparents', *Journal of Family Issues*, vol 22, no 4, pp 427-55.

Mueller, M.M., Wilhelm, B. and Elder, G.H. (2002) 'Variations in grandparenting', *Research on Aging*, vol 24, no 3, pp 360-88.

Mumford, A. (2001) 'Marketing working mothers: contextualizing earned income tax credits within feminist cultural theory', *Journal of Social Welfare and Family Law*, vol 23, pp 411-26.

Neugarten, B.L. and Weinstein, K.K. (1964) 'The changing American grandparent', *Journal of Marriage and the Family*, vol 26, pp 199-204.

O'Brien, M. and Jones, D. (1996) 'Young people's attitudes to fatherhood', in P. Moss (ed) *Father figures: Fathers in the families of the 1990s. Children in Scotland*, London: The Stationery Office.

Oeppen, J. and Vaupel, J.W. (2002) 'Enhanced-broken limits to life expectancy', *Science*, vol 296, May, pp 1029-31.

Olson, D., Russell, C. and Sprenkle, D. (1989) *Circumplex model: Systemic assessment and treatment of families*, New York, NY: Haworth Press.

Pearlin, L.I. (1982) 'Discontinuities in the study of ageing', in T.K. Hareven and K.J. Adams (eds) *Ageing and life course transitions: An interdisciplinary perspective*, London: Tavistock Publications.

Perry, A., Douglas, G., Murch, M., Bader, K. and Borkowski, M. (2000) *How parents cope financially on marriage breakdown*, London: Family Policy Studies Research Centre for the Joseph Rowntree Foundation.

Reimers, S. (1999) '"Good morning Sir", "Axe handle": talking at cross-purposes in family therapy', *Journal of Family Therapy*, vol 21, no 4, pp 360-76.

Richards, A. (2001) *Second time around: A survey of grandparents raising their grandchildren*, London: Family Rights Group.

Richards, A. and Tapsfield, R. (2003) *Funding family and friends care: The way forward*, London: Family Rights Group.

Rieff, P. (1959) *Freud: The mind of the moralist*, London: Methuen.

Riley, M.W. and Riley, J.W. (1993) 'Connections: kin and cohort', in V.L. Bengston and W.A. Achenbaum (eds) *The changing contract across generations*, New York, NY: Aldine de Gruyter.

Roberto, A.B., Allen, K.R. and Bleiszner, R. (2001) 'Grandfathers' perceptions and expectations of relationships with their adult grandchildren', *Journal of Family Issues*, vol 22, no 4, pp 407-26.

Roberto, K. and Stroes, J. (1992) 'Grandparents and grandchildren: roles, influences and relationships', *International Journal of Aging and Human Development*, vol 34, pp 227-39.

Robertson, J.F., Tice, C.H. and Loeb, L.L. (1985) 'Grandparenthood: from knowledge to programs and policy', in V.L. Bengtson and J.F. Robertson (eds) *Grandparenthood*, Beverly Hills, CA: Sage Publications.

Rodgers, B. and Pryor, J. (1998) *The development of children from separated families: A review of research from the United Kingdom*, York: Joseph Rowntree Foundation.

Rossi, A.S. and Rossi, P.H. (1990) *Of human bondings: Parent–child relations across the life course*, New York, NY: Aldine de Gruyter.

Schimoeller, G.L. and Baranowski, M.D. (1998) 'Intergenerational support in families with disabilities: grandparents' perspectives', *Families in Society*, vol 79, no 5, pp 465-76.

Silverstein, M. and Long, J.D. (1998) 'Trajectories of grandparents' perceived solidarity with adult grandchildren: a growth curve analysis over 23 years', *Journal of Marriage and the Family*, vol 60, November, pp 912-23.

Silverstein, M. and Marenco, M. (2001) 'How Americans enact the grandparent role across the family life course', *Journal of Family Issues*, vol 22, no 4, pp 493-522.

Silverstein, N.M. and Vehvilainen, L. (2000) 'Grandparents and schools: issues and potential challenges', in B. Cox (ed) *To grandmother's house we go and stay: Perspectives on custodial grandparents*, New York, NY: Springer Publishing Company.

Smart, C. and Neale, B. (1999) *Family fragments?*, Cambridge: Polity Press.

Smith, P.K. (1991) 'Introduction: the study of grandparenthood', in P.K. Smith (ed) *The psychology of grandparenthood: An international perspective*, London: Routledge.

Somary, K. and Stricker, G. (1998) 'Becoming a grandparent: a longitudinal study of expectations and early experiences as a function of sex and lineage', *The Gerontologist*, vol 38, no 1, pp 53-61.

Spitze, G. and Ward, R. (1998) 'Gender variations', in M.E. Szinovacz (ed) *Handbook on grandparenthood*, Connecticut, CT: Greenwood Press.

Spock, B. (1958) *Baby and child care*, London: Bodley Head.

The Stationery Office (1998) *Meeting the childcare challenge: A childcare strategy for Scotland: A framework and consultation document*, Cmd 3958, May.

Street, E. (1994) *Counselling for family problems*, London: Sage Publications.

Street, E. (1997) 'Family counselling', in S. Palmer and G. McMahon (eds) *Handbook of counselling* (2nd edn), London: Routledge.

Strom, R., Collinsworth, P., Strom, S. and Griswold, D. (1993) 'Strengths and needs of black grandparents', *International Journal of Aging and Human Development*, vol 36, pp 255-68.

Strom, R.D. and Strom, S.K. (1991) *Becoming a better grandparent: Viewpoints on strengthening the family*, Newbury Park, CA: Sage Publications.

Szinovacz, M.E. (1998) (ed) 'Grandparent research: past, present and future', in M.E. Szinovacz (ed) *Handbook on grandparenthood*, Connecticut, CT: Greenwood Press.

Szinovacz, M.E. and Roberts, A. (1998) 'Programs for grandparents', in M.E. Szinovacz (ed) *Handbook on grandparenthood*, Connecticut, CT: Greenwood Press.

Tein, J.-Y., Sandler, I.N. and Zautra, A.J. (2000) 'Stressful life events, psychological distress, coping and parenting of divorced mothers: a longitudinal study', *Journal of Family Psychology*, vol 14, no 1, pp 27-41.

Thibaut, J.W. and Kelley, H.H. (1959) *The social psychology of groups*, New York, NY: Wiley.

Thompson, G.G. (1952) *Child psychology*, Boston, MA: Houghton-Mifflin.

Thompson, P. (1999) 'The role of grandparents when parents part or die: some reflections on the mythical decline of the extended family', *Aging and Society*, vol 19, no 4, pp 471-503.

Tingle, N. (1990) *Grandparents? Who needs them?*, London: Family Rights Group.

Tinsley, B.J. and Parke, R.D. (1984) 'Grandparents as support and socialisation agents', in M. Lewis (ed) *Beyond the dyad*, New York, NY: Plenum.

Treas, J. (1995) 'Commentary: beanpole or beanstalk? Comments on "The demography of changing intergenerational relations"', in V.L. Bengtson, K.W. Schaie and L.M. Burton (eds) *Adult intergenerational relations*, New York, NY: Springer.

Troll, L.E. (1983) 'Grandparents: the 'family watchdogs', in T.H. Brubaker (ed) *Family relationships in later life*, Beverly Hills, CA: Sage Publications.

Troll, L.E. (1985) 'The contingencies of grandparenthood', in V.L. Bengtson and J.F. Robertson (eds) *Grandparenthood*, Beverly Hills, CA: Sage Publications.

Uhlenberg, P. and Hammill, B.G. (1998) 'Frequency of grandparent contact with grandchild sets: six factors that make a difference', *The Gerontologist*, vol 38, no 3, pp 276-85.

Uhlenberg, P. and Kirby, J.B. (1998) 'Grandparenthood over time: historical and demographic trends', in M.E. Szinovacz (ed) *Handbook on grandparenthood*, Connecticut, CT: Greenwood Press.

Vollmer, H. (1937) 'The grandmother: a problem in childrearing', *American Journal of Orthopsychiatry*, vol 7, pp 378-82.

Wallerstein, J. and Kelly, J.B. (1980) *Surviving the break-up: How children and parents cope with divorce*, New York, NY: Basic Books.

Weiss, R.S. (1979) 'Growing up a little faster: the experience of growing up in a single-parent household', *The Journal of Social Issues*, vol 35, no 4, pp 97-111.

Welsh Office (1998) *National childcare strategy in Wales: A consultation document*, June.

Werner, E.E. (1991) 'Grandchild–grandparent relationships amongst US ethnic groups', in P.K. Smith (ed) *The psychology of grandparenthood: An international perspective*, London: Routledge.

Yalom, I. (1995) *The theory and practice of group psychotherapy* (4th edn), New York, NY: Basic Books.

The families and the research methods

Choice of method

This research project took a qualitative approach. It emphasised the content of conversations and their hermeneutic analysis. This meant that the focus of attention was on the analysis of connected chunks of speech in the form of verbatim interview transcripts that were scrutinised for the presence of recurring themes and issues. Miles and Huberman (1994) have provided a list of what they see as the most important features of qualitative data. It includes features that influenced our decision to use qualitative methodology rather than postal questionnaires or interviews that might have sought answers to specific questions about grandparenting in divorced families. The most significant feature is what Miles and Huberman (1994, p 10) describe as "the inherent flexibility of qualitative data and their capacity to be varied as the study proceeds". This was important because our study set out with few specific questions in mind. It was planned as a piece of *exploratory* research and aimed to apply a Grounded Theory approach (see Chapter One) by checking whether predictions generated within the data were confirmed when more interview transcripts were available for analysis. Qualitative data analysis presented itself as the most appropriate approach and the best method to achieve the study's objectives (see Chapter One, p 4 of this book).

The families

The first group of parents that took part in the study was identified from divorce court records in six courts in South Wales and the West of England. Letters were sent to 162 parents who had divorced in 1997 and reminder letters were sent and telephone calls were made in an effort to boost the number that could be interviewed. Acceptances (see Table A1) were received from 36 parents in 34 different families and appointments were made to interview at least one parent in 29 different families. (Issues of cost, distance and a variety of other circumstances meant that some parents were not contacted.) All of these parents who had been granted a decree nisi in the first half of 1997 had participated in previous studies of divorce conducted by the university, but many had moved away and could not be contacted.

The study had been planned to include evidence from a sample of 40 families,

Table A1: Parents' response to the invitation to take part in the study

Parent group	Letters sent	Positive replies received from parents	Families interviewed
1997	162	36 (22%)	29
2000	472	64 (13%)	15
Total	634	100 (16%)	44

so more parents were needed to meet this target. Additional cases were identified from 240 divorce court files of couples that had been granted a decree nisi between March 2000 and September 2000. When these divorced couples were invited to take part in the research, 64 parents (a return of 13% of parents) accepted without the need for follow-up by letter or telephone call. This provided a point of contact with 59 different divorced families (25% of families) and 15 of these families were chosen to take part in the research. The selection was made by talking to parents on the telephone and using the information provided to select families in which it seemed likely that grandparents as well as parents could be interviewed.

In the two groups that were drawn from the court records, almost 70% of parents were divorcing after the breakdown of their first marriage. In 24% of couples, one of the spouses had been previously married, and in just under 8% of cases, both spouses had been married before. The median length of the marriages was 11 years. Three quarters of the petitioners for divorce were women. The couples that divorced in 1997 were most frequently divorced at ages 30-34 but those in 2000 were most frequently divorced between 35 and 37 years of age. The difference is probably explained by the fact that a higher proportion of the parents who divorced in 2000 had been married before. It was not possible to generate reliable data on the social class of parents from the information held in the court files. An analysis of the data from the court file demonstrated that the characteristics of parents who agreed to take part in the study did not differ significantly from those of the whole sample.

A total of 115 interviews with family members was completed. These consisted of interviews with 33 mothers, 16 fathers and 30 children (see Table 1 of this book). There were 35 resident parents (33 mothers and two fathers) and 21 maternal grandparents and 15 paternal grandparents were interviewed. Twenty-six interviews were with grandparents in their sixties or seventies; seven were with grandparents in their fifties; two were with grandparents in their eighties, and one was with a 49-year-old grandmother who was the only grandparent who was interviewed who had full-time care of her grandchildren.

Recruiting family members to take part in the study

Our strategy was to use our initial contacts with the parents to help arrange interviews with other family members. Chapter One discussed some of the reasons why it proved difficult to persuade parents to take part in the research. Family relationships after a divorce is a sensitive subject and parents perceived our investigation to be intrusive. Some expressed a fear that their participation might upset their ex-spouse and many preferred not to provide addresses, telephone numbers or information about the grandparents on the other side of the divorced family (see Chapter One). Most parents, however, did not offer an explanation of their reasons for refusing to take part in the research.

The two interviewers who carried out the interviews were also engaged in persuading parents to take part. One was male and the other female. When the success rate of the two interviewers was examined, it was found that their 'hit rate', or proportion of successes with the 1997 group of parents, was almost identical. It was concluded that the interviewers' gender, personal style or the manner of their approach to parents by telephone could not account for the problems that were encountered in recruiting parents, grandparents and grandchildren.

Method

The aim was to interview both parents, one of the divorced couple's children aged 8-16, and the maternal and paternal grandparents. Parents with care of children were asked whether or not a member of the research team could talk to one of their children (selected at random where there was more than one child in the appropriate age range). This child then became the focus of attention in the interviews with grandparents. When an interviewer was refused permission to talk to a grandchild, the parent and grandparent interviews still focused on a randomly selected 'target child'. The letter inviting parents and grandparents to take part offered them an interview fee of £20. Grandchildren who agreed to be interviewed were sent a certificate and a pen with the university logo.

However, due to the difficulties we encountered in talking to family members on both sides of the divorced family (particularly when there was continuing acrimony and unresolved conflict) there was only one complete family in which a grandchild, both parents and both sets of grandparents were interviewed. There were seven families in which it was possible to complete four interviews. There were 14 cases in which three interviews took place (often the mother, the child and the maternal grandparents), 18 in which there were only two interviews and four families in which it was only possible to talk to one parent.

The interview

A flexible 'conversational-style' interview was chosen as the research tool, since we aimed to encourage family members to talk about the issues that they felt were important to them (see Chapter One). It was based on three interview guides (see Table A3) that ensured that the two interviewers covered much the same ground. The interviews for adults usually lasted between one and two

Table A2: The family members who were interviewed

Target grandchild's name	1997 sample					
	Mothers	Fathers	Grand-children	Maternal grandparents	Paternal grandparents	Totals
Alan	*		*	*		3
Linda	*		*			2
Robert	*		*	*		3
Debbie		*	*		*	3
Alfie	*		*			2
Irene	*		*	*	*	4
Glynis	*		*			2
Marion	*		*	*		3
Carl	*			*		2
Clare	*		*			2
Helen	*	*	*	*		4
Edward	*		*	*		3
Diana	*		*	*		3
Valerie	*		*			2
Belinda		*	*		*	3
Susan	*		*			2
Jane	*		*	*	*	4
William	*					1
Kate	*		*			2
Barbara	*		*			2
Eleanor	*		*	*		3
Pat		*			*	2
Tom		*				1
Annabel		*			*	2
Oliver		*			*	2
Zoe		*				1
George	*	*				2
Charles	*		*	*	*	4
Frank	*					1
Total	22	9	20	11	8	70

	2000 sample					
	Mothers	Fathers	Grand-children	Maternal grandparents	Paternal grandparents	Totals
Ingrid	*	*	*	*	*	5
Janet	*		*	*		3
Karen	*	*	*	*		4
Len	*		*	*		3
Norman	*		*	*		3
Elizabeth	*		*	*		3
Steve	*		*	*	*	4
Tony	*		*			2
Wendy	*		*	*		3
Peter	*		*	*		3
Martin		*			*	2
Pauline		*			*	2
Robin		*			*	2
Ann	*	*		*	*	4
Brian		*			*	2
Total	11	7	10	10	7	45

Table A3: The interview guides

Grandparent	Parent	Grandchild
Current relationships with the family and grandchildren	Contacts with family	Relationship with maternal grandparents
Activities with grandchildren	Your parents' relationship with your children	Activities with maternal grandparents
History of relationship with the divorced family	Differences between grandmother's and grandfather's relationship with grandchildren	Relationships with paternal and/or step-grandparents
Effect of divorce on relationship with own child, ex-child-in-law and grandchildren.	Ex-parents-in-law relationships with their grandchildren	Views on grandparents and discipline
Provision of help at the time of the divorce	Grandparents and discipline	Sibling's relationship with grandparents
Communications and decision making	Grandparents' pastoral role	Contact with grandparents before the divorce
Divorced couple's new partners	Provision of help at the time of the divorce	Grandparents' pastoral role
Legal aspects	Grandparents' opinion about your choice of spouse	Provision of help from grandparents
Questions concerning the following were then asked of grandmothers and grandfathers separately:	Family relations and new partners	Characteristics of good grandparents
1. Relationships with grandchildren	Legal aspects	Legal aspects
2. Expectations of the grandparent role		
3. Adult children		

hours. Parents, grandparents and grandchildren were met in their own home, assured of the confidential nature of the interview and asked whether a tape recorder could be used during the interview. Grandparents who lived together were interviewed together. However, at the end of each interview they were interviewed separately for about ten minutes so that the data could be explored for differences between grandmothers' and grandfathers' grandparenting practices. This also gave grandparents the opportunity to provide opinions that were not influenced by the presence of their spouse. Resident parents were asked whether or not a child could be interviewed alone and children's interviews usually lasted about 30 minutes. These interviews began after children of all ages had used a box of cardboard figures to explain who was in the family and where they lived. This not only helped to put the grandchild at ease but also provided a very useful starting point for a discussion about grandparents on both sides of the divorced family.

Qualitative data analysis

All interviews were transcribed and each transcription was analysed using the computer programme ATLAS.ti. The programme allows researchers to reduce a large volume of text to a more manageable set of codes that represent the researchers' interpretation of the respondents' comments (for example, 'Grandchild expresses affection for grandparent','Grandparent expresses negative feelings about ex-child-in-law', and so on). These codes can be grouped in families and interpreted as sets of interrelated ideas. The software allows the researcher to produce web-like diagrams showing hypothesised relationships between codes, and to 'play' with the data and interpret it. As a result of this process of interpretation, we were able to generate a list of 'emerging themes and issues' for discussion by the research team. Our analysis aimed to determine whether specific predictions generated *within* the data held up when they were tested across a larger number of cases. The process supported the development of 'Grounded Theory' (see Chapter One).

Qualitative studies (Miles and Huberman, 1994) focus on naturally occurring, ordinary events in natural settings and hold the possibility of generating ideas that the research team would not otherwise have thought of raising with the informants. Important issues are not always capable of being anticipated and, sometimes, traditional approaches can prove inadequate in tackling research that expects to encounter a wide diversity of behaviour and attitudes. For example, a grandparent–grandchild relationship that might be rated as 'wholly satisfactory' by the majority of respondents to a postal questionnaire or semi-structured interview, might include grandparents who enjoy occasional contact with their grandchildren and those that share confidences and have a deep level of affection and understanding. Correlation studies that relate the quality or quantity of grandparent–grandchild contact to a variety of other variables pay less attention to the internal dynamics of the relationship. The strengths and limitations of our qualitative study that explored the relationships of three generations of divorced families are discussed in Chapter One.

Index

A

activities with grandparents 33-46
  adult-centred activities 22, 34-5, 40,
    41, 131-2
  adult-centred/child-centred continuum
    22, 34-5, 40, 41, 45-6, 131-2
  affectionate relationships 35-6, 38,
    132-3, 142
  grandparent gender differences 65-8
African-American grandparents 18, 19
age of grandparents and grandchildren
  research on 18-19
  see also older grandchildren; older
    grandparents
Aldous, J. 1, 11, 16
Allen, K.R. 9, 14
altruism 11
Amato, P.R. 9
Aquilino, W.S. 9
Arthur, S. 6-7, 11, 76, 135
'asymmetrical' relationships 24, 32, 133,
  142

B

Beck, U. 4
Beck-Gernsheim, E. 4
Bengtson, V.L. 1, 35
'better grandparenting' 133, 136-9
black grandparents 18, 19
Booth, A.K. 10
'boring' visits 36, 40, 41-2, 43, 44
Boszormenghnagy, I. 12
Brown, J. 82
Burghes, L. 14

C

Campbell, L. 84
carers
  grandparents as main carers 73, 77,
    134
  see also childcare provision
Chan, C.G. 57
Cherlin, A.J. 12, 13, 17, 18, 19, 36, 71-2,
  105, 142
child development: discipline 15
child-centred activities see adult-
  centred/child-centred activities

childcare practices 2
  see also discipline by grandparents
childcare provision
  and ethnicity 18
  and family policy 3-4, 76-7, 134-5,
    142-3
  grandparent hierarchy 61-3
  grandparents as surrogate parents
    109-13, 118-19, 132
  grandparents as main carers 73, 77,
    134
  paternal grandparents 61-3
  payment for childcare 3, 134-5
  reservations of grandparents 109-13,
    142
  support for 136-9
  obligation and affection 104-5, 142-3
  resistance to 16, 28, 106, 134
  see also reluctant grandparents
children see grandchildren
Children Act (1989) 72-3, 74, 75
Clingempeel, W.G. 65
close relationships see emotional
  closeness
communication in divorced families
  79-88
  confiding in grandparents 29-31, 35,
    39-40
  feedback from grandchildren 84-7,
    132
  'non-communication norm' 83, 87,
    88, 132, 133-4, 139-40
  counselling for divorced families
    139-40
  parent/grandparent communications
    79-85, 133
  professional view of 87-8
confiding in grandparents 29-31, 35,
  39-40
contact
  importance of 141-2
  incidence see frequency of contact
  legal position 72-4, 75, 122-6, 128-30,
    134, 140-1
  see also excluded grandparents
'contact orders' 72-3, 75, 122-4, 134,
  140
Cooney, T.M. 12, 14
coping methods 83, 87, 140
corporal punishment 50-1

Also available from The Policy Press

Families and work in the twenty-first century

Shirley Dex

This review draws together the findings from 20 individual JRF research projects, published in the Family and Work series. It covers a wide range of issues including childcare, caring for older relatives, employment and self-employment, flexible working, working unsociable hours and the ability to move with a job. Together with important insights into where both families and employers feel most pressure, this overview reflects on whether recent government policy, aimed at helping working families is moving in the right direction. It provides a comprehensive overview of the way families relate to the labour market at a time of considerable policy change.

Paperback £16.95 (US$28.95) ISBN 1 85935 095 X
297 x 210mm 108 pages September 2003

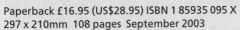

Families in conflict

Perspectives of children and parents on the Family Court Welfare Service

Ann Buchanan, Joan Hunt, Harriet Bretherton and Victoria Bream

This report is published at a critical time in the development of services to families involved in court disputes about children. As the new Children and Family Court Advisory and Support Service (CAFCASS) takes over responsibility for the work previously undertaken by family court welfare officers, the experiences of the parents and children reported in this study will provide an invaluable service user perspective for the benefit of policy and practice.

Paperback £16.99 (US$29.95) ISBN 1 86134 333 7
297 x 210mm 128 pages November 2001

Seven years in the lives of British families
Evidence on the dynamics of social change from the British Household Panel Survey

Richard Berthoud and Robert Gershuny

This groundbreaking study provides important new insights into the dynamics of Britain's social and economic life – in family structures and relationships; in employment and household incomes; in housing, health and political affiliations. A total of 10,000 adults (from 5,500 households) were interviewed every year between 1991 and 1997, providing a unique picture of the processes and outcomes of important events in their lives.

Paperback £19.99 (US$32.50) ISBN 1 86134 200 4
Hardback £50.00 (US$75.00) ISBN 1 86134 201 2
216 x 148mm 256 pages November 2000

Senior citizenship?
Retirement, migration and welfare in the European Union

Louise Ackers and Peter Dwyer

Debates about citizenship in Europe, particularly in relation to social policy and welfare provision, are increasingly topical as the European Union expands and moves towards greater integration. This book charts the development of mobility and welfare rights for retired people moving or returning home under the Free Movement of Persons provisions. It raises important issues around the future of social citizenship and the implications of the exercise of agency, in an increasingly global and mobile world.

Paperback £21.99 (US$37.50) ISBN 1 86134 264 0
234 x 156mm 232 pages June 2002

Transitions after 50 series

Published in association with the Joseph Rowntree Foundation
This topical new series explores people's experiences, decisions and constraints as they pass from active labour market participation in their middle years towards a new identity in later life. For more information about individual titles, please visit our website at **www.policypress.org.uk**

JR
JOSEPH
ROWNTREE
FOUNDATION

Crossroads after 50
Improving choices in work and retirement
Donald Hirsch

This report draws together the findings from 12 individual Joseph Rowntree Foundation Research Projects, published in the Transitions after 50 series.

With critical implications for shaping policy, *Crossroads after 50* brings to the attention of the policy and research communities revealing findings from a previously under-researched field.

Paperback £18.99 (US$23.95) ISBN 1 85935 155 7
297 x 210mm 60 pages December 2003

To order further copies of this publication or any other Policy Press titles please contact:

In the UK and Europe:
Marston Book Services, PO Box 269, Abingdon, Oxon, OX14 4YN, UK
Tel: +44 (0)1235 465500, Fax: +44 (0)1235 465556,
Email: direct.orders@marston.co.uk

In the USA and Canada:
ISBS, 920 NE 58th Street, Suite 300, Portland, OR 97213-3786, USA
Tel: +1 800 944 6190 (toll free), Fax: +1 503 280 8832,
Email: info@isbs.com

In Australia and New Zealand:
DA Information Services, 648 Whitehorse Road, Mitcham, Victoria 3132, Australia
Tel: +61 (3) 9210 7777, Fax: +61 (3) 9210 7788,
E-mail: service@dadirect.com.au

Further information about all of our titles can be also be found on our website:

www.policypress.org.uk